1931

TOBIAS STRAUMANN

1931

DEBT, CRISIS, AND THE RISE OF HITLER

OXFORD
UNIVERSITY PRESS

OXFORD

UNIVERSITY PRESS

Great Clarendon Street, Oxford, ox2 6DP,
United Kingdom

Oxford University Press is a department of the University of Oxford.
It furthers the University's objective of excellence in research, scholarship,
and education by publishing worldwide. Oxford is a registered trade mark of
Oxford University Press in the UK and in certain other countries

First Edition published in 2019

Impression: 1

Published in the United States of America by Oxford University Press
198 Madison Avenue, New York, NY 10016, United States of America

British Library Cataloguing in Publication Data
Data available

Library of Congress Control Number: 2018965383

ISBN 978–0–19–881618–8

Printed and bound in Great Britain by
Clays Ltd, Elcograf S.p.A.

PREFACE

This is a book about one of the most important events of modern times; the German financial crisis of 1931. In the summer of that year, parts of the German banking system collapsed, the government stopped servicing some of its foreign debts, and the free convertibility of the German currency was abruptly suspended. These shocks triggered a global liquidity crisis, the destruction of the gold-based international monetary system, and a severe banking crisis in the United States, turning the worldwide recession into a depression. The German financial crisis of 1931 also had devastating political consequences, undermining the established democratic parties and enabling Hitler's rise to power.

The idea to write this book grew out of my belief that the wider public has little knowledge of the 1931 German financial crisis and its key role in Hitler's sudden electoral success. But the immediate spur to action came from my unease observing the intense debates surrounding the euro crisis that erupted in Greece in 2010 and spilled over to other southern European countries and Ireland. As in the 1930s, a doomed loop of activity involving sovereign debt, private debt, bank failures, and a deficient monetary system led to a financial crisis that shook—and, in my view, continues to shake—Western Europe's political foundations.

The relevance of the German financial crisis of 1931 for today's debates goes beyond this obvious parallel, however. The fundamental cause of the German crisis was the inability of the parties to resolve the demands of international agreements with those of domestic political realities. The victors of the First World War aimed to design a reparations scheme that punished Germany without crushing it, and in order to reach this goal, many well-meaning diplomats and politicians tried several times to make the scheme more tolerable to Germany, ending with the so-called Young Plan in 1930. But, the negotiators of the Young Plan failed to take adequate account of the rapidly deteriorating economic and political situation in Germany. The recession which began in 1929 was forcing Chancellor Heinrich Brüning's government repeatedly to lower wages, cut spending, and raise taxes in order to service its reparations and other foreign debts, exacerbating the recession and playing directly into Hitler's hands.

Hitler revelled in blaming foreign powers for Germany's economic difficulties. And, as nearly all Weimar politicians were unhappy with the reparations regime, they rebutted his arguments only half-heartedly. Of course, his criticisms were exaggerated, and it goes without saying that other factors contributed to his success—Hitler's charisma and political talent, the anti-Semitic climate, his stand against Bolshevism, his emphatic nationalism, and his messianic promise to unite the German people. Nevertheless, when analysing his speeches and electoral campaigns, one is struck by the success of his relentless denunciations of the reparations regime. Foreign debt, austerity, and the rise of Hitler were closely intertwined.

To develop this narrative, I have drawn ideas from many conversations with friends and colleagues. The most important of these were Markus Diem Meier, Markus Somm, and Oliver Zimmer. They forced me to sharpen the argument and explain the relevance of a past financial crisis. In addition, Oliver, one of the most astute observers of social shifts and their political implications I know, was the first to encourage me to go beyond the economic aspects of the 1931 financial crisis. His constant support proved crucial for completing the project. I also profited enormously from exchanges with economic historians who share my strong interest in the 1931 crisis: Olivier Accominotti, Alexander Apostolides, Johannes Bähr, Simon Banholzer, Vincent Bignon, Øyvind Eitrheim, Marc Flandreau, Juan Flores, Luca Froelicher, Per Hansen, Clemens Jobst, Lars Jonung, Drew Keeling, Jan Tore Klovland, Peter Kugler, Matthias Morys, Lars Ögren, Lars Fredrik Øksendal, Mary O'Sullivan, Gianluca Pardini, Alexander Rathke, Alfred Reckendrees, Samad Sarferaz, Mark Spoerer, Stefano Ugolini, Scott Urban, Hans-Joachim Voth, Florian Weber, Ulrich Woitek, and Nikolaus Wolf. I owe special thanks to Harold James and Albrecht Ritschl whose endorsement proved crucial for finalizing the book. Finally, I am indebted to Ian Rodger for making this book readable for an English audience and helping me clarify my thoughts, and Luciana O'Flaherty and her staff at Oxford University Press for their excellent management and support.

CONTENTS

CONTENTS

LIST OF MAPS

LIST OF FIGURES

LIST OF ILLUSTRATIONS

LIST OF TABLES

ABBREVIATIONS

ADAP	Akten zur deutschen auswärtigen Politik
AdR	Akten der Reichskanzlei
DBFP	Documents on British Foreign Policy
DDP	Deutsche Demokratische Partei (German Democratic Party)
DNVP	Deutschnationale Volkspartei (German National People's Party)
DVP	Deutsche Volkspartei (German People's Party)
FRUS	Papers relating to the Foreign Relations of the United States
KPD	Kommunistische Partei Deutschlands (Communist Party of Germany)
NSDAP (a.k.a. Nazis)	Nationalsozialistische Deutsche Arbeiterpartei (National Socialist German Workers' Party)
NYT	*The New York Times*
OHL	Oberste Heeresleitung
SA	Sturmabteilung (Storm Troops)
SPD	Sozialdemokratische Partei Deutschlands (Social Democratic Party of Germany)
VZ	*Vossische Zeitung*

INTRODUCTION

On 14 July 1931, Joseph Goebbels, leader of the NSDAP (Nationalsozialistische Deutsche Arbeiterpartei) Berlin branch and party propaganda chief, was exultant. 'The craziest things happen in politics', he wrote in his diary. 'The credits have dried up. Chancellor Brüning has run into serious problems. The Reich is verging on bankruptcy. Our hour approaches with eeric certainty, and we will seize it. After Brüning, it is our turn.'[1]

Sadly, Goebbels was right. Germany's financial crisis precipitated the collapse of the Weimar Republic with frightening speed. Only eighteen months later, in January 1933, Hitler was named Chancellor by President Hindenburg. Goebbels may have been wrong in predicting that the Nazis would overtake the government immediately after Brüning—two other figures, Franz von Papen and Kurt von Schleicher, sat briefly in the Chancellery before Hitler came to power—but Goebbels's basic intuition was correct. A government that shuts down banks, introduces capital controls, and declares partial default in the middle of a deep slump has little chance of surviving. Brüning managed to stay in power until May 1932, but after July 1931 he was mortally wounded.

Germany's 1931 financial crisis not only gave the Nazis the opening they needed, but also triggered an international liquidity crisis, throwing banks and financial markets across the globe into chaos. Panicked investors forced sterling to go off the gold standard, prompting a wave of devaluations in such distant places as

India and Japan, a run on the dollar, and a banking crisis in the United States. Like dominoes, the pillars of the global economy toppled one after another. It was not the stock market crash of 1929 that pushed the world into economic depression, but the German crisis of 1931. This in turn further weakened the German economy and the government in Berlin.

Every generation since has studied this extraordinary period of political and economic havoc.[2] Now that we are emerging from another great financial crisis and living in a world of political polarization, it seems a particularly appropriate moment to revisit the events of 1931. The central question that needs to be answered has remained the same ever since it happened: why weren't policy-makers able to prevent such a disaster?

A common hypothesis is that they did not see it coming, and there is some truth to that. Early warnings expressed by independent economists were ignored, and many politicians indulged themselves in moralistic lecturing that lacked basic economic literacy. Yet, after the currency crisis triggered by the sensational victory of the Nazi Party in the September 1930 Reichstag elections, many politicians realized that Germany was on the brink of financial collapse. From that moment, they had plenty of time to prevent the disaster from happening. So cognitive inertia explains only part of the drama.

But if policymakers became aware of what was at stake, what took them so long to act? Did they lack the courage to take tough decisions? Again, there is some evidence to support this view, as, undoubtedly, the politicians in charge were not extraordinary statesmen. But when we study the biographies of Western political leaders of that era, they do not appear particularly cowardly or incompetent. US President Herbert Hoover was an intelligent and experienced administrator with a great understanding of Europe's problems. The British Prime Minister Ramsay MacDonald showed a deep interest in international cooperation, eager to build bridges to ease tensions. French foreign policy was in the hands of Aristide Briand, one of the most able diplomats to have served France. And the German Chancellor Heinrich Brüning was considered a judicious politician and one of the leading experts in fiscal policy at the time. Of course, they all made mistakes, especially Brüning, but it is hard to argue that a different set of politicians would have easily defused the ticking bomb.

Another hypothesis highlights the institutional framework within which politicians operated. This appears to be the most plausible explanation. In the early 1930s, the German government had almost no room for manoeuvre because of its heavy foreign debt burden. Not only did it have to pay reparations for the First World War, it was also heavily indebted to foreign banks in the wake of a borrowing frenzy during the boom years of the late 1920s. When the world economic crisis took hold, the German government had no choice but to pursue austerity policies that further deepened the recession and required several rounds of spending cuts and tax increases. Furthermore, the gold standard made it difficult to provide sufficient liquidity to the banking system. The German central bank was required to hold a minimum of 40 per cent gold and foreign exchange reserve against all notes in circulation. It was only a matter of time, in these pernicious circumstances, before radical parties would win elections and the financial and monetary system would collapse.[3]

It is obvious that creditors, both private and public, could and should have relieved Germany of its obligations, and there were important voices demanding just that. But for understandable reasons, politicians in France, Great Britain, and the USA hesitated and opted for a gradual diplomatic approach. The memory of the Great War was still fresh, governments distrusted each other, and domestic public opinion in key countries was sceptical about far-reaching concessions and debt cancellations. Moreover, the crisis deepened with great speed, overwhelming the everyday routine of politics and diplomacy. Eventually, at the eleventh hour, US President Hoover started an initiative to stop the run on the German currency. But it was too late to prevent the 1931 financial crisis.

Thus, the German crisis is instructive not because it shows that politicians sometimes fail to act courageously. That is to be expected. Most of us like to play safe. Rather, it teaches us a time-less lesson about the importance of getting international agree-ments right. In the 1920s, the Allies failed to come up with a reparation regime corresponding to the economic and political realities in Germany. True, diplomats and politicians tried hard to adjust the regime to changing circumstances, holding nearly thirty specially convened conferences and agreeing on the Dawes Plan of 1924 and then the Young Plan of 1930. But a study of the proceedings of the 1920s conferences reveals little evidence of an awareness of the urgent need for a new, more realistic approach. 'The politically practicable and the economically possible were at war', a contemporary observer aptly summarized the tragedy unfolding between 1919 and 1931. 'The struggle was like some long drawn out conflict on a hill-side, where political forces endeav-oured repeatedly to advance uphill, and on occasion even suc-ceeded in doing so for a time, while the prevailing economic factors drove them steadily downhill.'[4]

The following account will focus on the most dramatic period between January 1930, when the Young Plan was concluded, and July 1931 when the financial crisis erupted. We will see in Part I how most bankers, diplomats, and politicians were slow in deciphering the magnitude of what was happening. Part II describes the turning points that made them understand what was at stake and how they tried to work around the constraints. Part III describes the ultimate failure to avert the disaster and the rapid deterioration of the financial crisis. It is a story of almost biblical proportions, demonstrating how quickly a situation that seems manageable at first can spin out of control.

PART I

CONFIDENCE

1

LAUGHING AT THE RAVEN

In January 1930, the Viennese economist Felix Somary travelled to the University of Heidelberg to give a talk about the prospects for the world economy. Somary was one of the most respected analysts of his time. Whenever a crisis loomed, ministers, central bankers, and business leaders—from the Austrian Rothschild family to the President of the Reichsbank, Hjalmar Schacht, and the Social Democratic Finance Minister, Rudolf Hilferding—would seek out what Somary had to say. He called himself 'a political meteorologist' and earned his living as a partner in a small private bank, Blankart & Cie., in Zurich. His financial independence allowed him to say what he really thought about the state of the world.[1]

His friends in Heidelberg wanted to know whether the recent stock market crash on Wall Street marked the beginning of a serious economic slowdown in Europe. Somary himself had witnessed Black Thursday (24 October 1929) in New York, when the market had lost more than 10 per cent of its value in one day. He was alarmed by the collapse of confidence and immediately cabled to his partners in Zurich: 'Keep clients out of the market. Crisis just beginning.' He was even more shocked by what happened a month later in Europe. Within weeks, the second largest Austrian bank, the Bodencreditanstalt, became insolvent, and the second largest Belgian bank, the Banque de Bruxelles, suffered a massive write-down of its assets stemming from the stock market crash.[2]

The message Somary delivered to his audience in Heidelberg was dire. 'I am convinced that what happened in November in Vienna and Brussels is the beginning of the most severe crisis in a century—only the beginning, the first act, and that we will not exit from this crisis within weeks or months, but in years. The collapse of the Bodencreditanstalt and the reconstruction of the Banque de Bruxelles were only summer lightning; we will witness failures of much greater proportions.'

Why was Somary so pessimistic? To him, these two bank failures were not isolated events, but symptoms of fundamental international imbalances that were about to unwind in a chaotic way. After the Great War, the Allied powers had decided to uphold the war debt claims against each other and to punish Germany with a high reparations bill. According to Somary, this agreement was a recipe for disaster. 'What drives us into the crisis? There is an enormous amount of insoluble debt. The European countries are supposed to pay their war debts to the United States, and because nobody knows how this transfer is supposed to work in the long run, the whole sum has been charged on Germany as reparation debt.'

The reason this pile of debt had not yet collapsed was that it had been stabilized by private short-term capital flows to Germany. But according to Somary, these additional loans only made things worse. 'The impossibility of servicing these debts is veiled by a system of short-term loans which have been granted to an extent that cannot be justified on financial grounds. In order to obtain these loans, agriculture and industry in the debtor countries are forced to consent to high interest rates which they will never be able to cover from their earnings. It is at this weakest link where the collapse will and must occur.' Banks providing loans would not be able to withstand the storm. 'The commercial and mortgage banks base their business on the solvency of their debtors, and the banks of the creditor countries on the solvency of the debtor banks.' In both cases, solvency was a fiction and the international financial structure stood like a house of cards.

Little time was left to avert total collapse, Somary warned. 'The danger that the chain holding together national and international economies will rip apart is nearer than one would think. Perhaps reparations and international political debts will eventually disappear in the vortex of the crisis, but it is highly probable that international private debts will also be hit on a scale unseen in generations.' Germany would be in a particularly dangerous situation once the downward spiral began. 'The deeper the crisis, the more difficult it will be to refinance short-term debts and the bigger the danger of a withdrawal of foreign funds and, hence, international insolvency.'

There was one remaining strategy that could rebalance the system, Somary concluded, and that was to bring about close Franco-German cooperation. 'If this does not happen, we will witness the whole apparatus of foreign exchange control, import and export bans, and at the end maybe not again inflation, but something that tears the fabric of the economy even more apart: the collapse of the banks and of public finances.'[3]

As we know, it didn't happen, and Somary (Illustration 1) was proved to be absolutely right. The Wall Street crash and the banking problems in Austria and Belgium were not temporary disturbances, but the beginning of the worst economic crisis of modern times. From

Illustration 1. Felix Somary, photo taken in the late 1930s.

1929 to 1932, world industrial production declined by 36 per cent and did not achieve the levels of 1929 until 1937. Unemployment grew to double-digit levels, while prices of raw materials and manufactured goods fell by 56 and 36 per cent respectively. World trade contracted by two-thirds in real terms. Somary also correctly identified Germany as the weakest link whose financial collapse would precipitate a dramatic downturn of the global economy. Between 1929 and 1932, German industrial production fell by almost 50 per cent. Unemployment reached more than 20 per cent, and in the industrial sector it went above 30 per cent. Real GDP shrank by roughly 25 per cent, real GDP per head by 17 per cent. And as Somary had foreseen, with the deepening of the crisis, reparations and war debts were eventually curtailed or cancelled and Germany's debts to foreign banks were frozen. The global economy broke up into several currency and trade blocs, bringing an end to an era of globalization.[4]

Why was Somary able to predict the economic collapse with such accuracy? One reason was his background. He was a well-trained economist with a rich practical experience as a banker and political adviser. He had studied at the University of Vienna and worked as an assistant to Carl Menger, a leading economist of his time. In 1905, when Somary was 24, he went to work for the Anglo-Austrian Bank, a Viennese institution founded by prominent bankers of the City of London, among them Sir Ernest Cassel. He acted as assistant to the managing director and took part in almost every important transaction. The 'Anglobank', as it was called, was active in corporate finance in Eastern Europe and the Balkans, requiring Somary to develop a deep knowledge of political and social conditions in that particularly turbulent corner of Europe. In 1909, he went to Berlin to work as an independent lecturer, banker, and adviser to the German government, gaining further insight into the inner workings of European politics and diplomacy. During the First World War, he and the famous sociologist Max Weber drafted a memorandum for Emperor Wilhelm II arguing against the escalation of submarine warfare.[5] After the First World War, he rescued the fortune of the Austrian Rothschild family by bringing it to the small private bank Blankart & Cie. in Zurich. Soon thereafter Somary was made a partner.

Another reason why Somary was able to make precise predictions was that he was gifted with a sixth sense for looming catastrophes. One of his friends, the Swiss diplomat Carl Jacob Burckhardt, observed in a letter to the Austrian writer Hugo von Hofmannsthal: 'There is a curious guy whom you also know, this Somary…He is one of those people who foresees crises; he is also clear-sighted when it comes to politics. All the predictions that I have heard from him have come to pass, some of them in an entirely amazing way.' Somary once told his son: 'I sense the future in my bones; it is not only about knowledge. It is signalled not in my head, but in my marrow.'[6]

For all his talent, Somary had no 'insider' knowledge. All he did was connect the dots. By the early 1930s, it was obvious there were huge international imbalances. The United States was the biggest creditor, Germany was the biggest debtor (Fig. 1.1). Belgium, France, Great Britain, and Italy had more-or-less even foreign debt balances, but their accounts depended on Germany's willingness and capacity to pay reparations to them. The Allied powers and Germany formed a chain, tied together by 'a colossal structure of inter-Governmental obligations', as *The Economist* observed.[7]

It was also well known that the German Reich, the German state governments, municipalities, banks, and corporations had borrowed huge amounts of private funds, especially from Wall

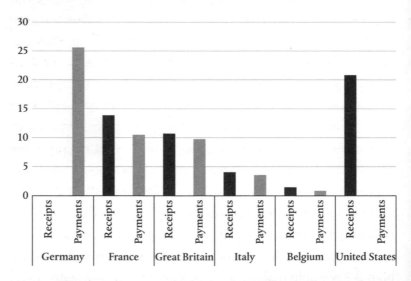

Fig. 1.1 All inter-governmental debts outstanding on 1 July 1931 (in billions of US dollars)

Street, to finance economic expansion and pay a large part of the reparations bill. By the end of 1929, debts owed to foreign banks amounted to RM 31 million—equivalent to about a third of German GDP at the time. Including the reparation obligations, the Reich had foreign debts amounting to a staggering 86 per cent of German GDP. And a considerable proportion of these foreign loans was short-term that needed to be repaid within a few weeks or months. By the late 1920s, banks, corporations, and the German authorities had become highly vulnerable to the volatile sentiments of investors.[8]

Why were the Germans increasing their foreign debt burden in addition to the reparations bill? Demand for foreign funds resulted, in part, from the lack of domestic credit and the undercapitalization of corporations in the wake of the 1923 hyperinflation. It was also due to the German government's inability to agree a budget surplus and earn a current account surplus. The weak Weimar Republic needed public support to survive the turbulent post-war years, and that could only be maintained by increasing public services and paying decent wages. Borrowing from abroad enabled the authorities to avoid unpopular tax increases, keep workers well paid, and postpone the true costs of reconstruction. Weimar was a 'mortgaged democracy', as one historian put it. City mayors, such as Konrad Adenauer in Cologne, were wont to launch big infrastructure projects—subways, bridges, parks, swimming pools, concert halls, and football stadiums—to boost voter loyalty.[9]

Another reason for Germany's borrowing was that some officials in the German Foreign Ministry saw an advantage in accumulating commercial debt owed to US banks. They argued that high debts would make it more probable that reparations would be cancelled as soon as the Reich threatened to default on its debts to private investors. Foreign Minister Gustav Stresemann explained in a speech in 1925: 'One must simply have enough debts; one must have so many debts that the creditor sees his own existence endangered if the debtor collapses . . . Such measures build bridges of political understanding and future political support.' A senior official at the German Foreign Ministry wrote in a memorandum in 1927: 'The higher our private debt, the smaller our reparations.'[10]

Finally, many American banks and, to a lesser extent, British, Dutch, and Swiss banks simply loved the business. They got higher returns from investments in Germany than from their domestic markets, and there was a general sense that it was a safe investment.[11] Germany was still Europe's most powerful economy, destined to recover from the ravages of war in due time. To be sure, Germany's burdens from the war were enormous. Two million of her soldiers had died on the battlefield, more than the losses of any other belligerent country. More than 4 million German soldiers had been wounded, with many them severely handicapped for the rest of their lives. And nearly 1 million German civilians had died. In addition, the Treaty of Versailles forced Germany to cede Alsace-Lorraine to France and some eastern areas to the newly created Polish nation. It also stripped the country of its overseas possessions, expropriated German property abroad, and placed the Saar valley and its coal-mining enterprises under French administration for fifteen years (Map 1). Yet, Germany was not economically crippled. The industrial base was intact as the war had not spread to German territory. German manufacturers continued to be leaders in coal, iron, and steel production, electrical engineering, chemical industry, and car making.[12]

The recovery was kick-started by the restoration of the gold-based German currency in 1924, and that minimized the exchange

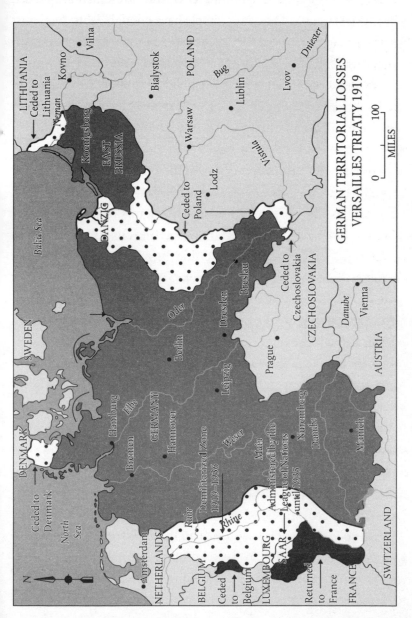

Map 1. Germany after the Treaty of Versailles

rate risk for foreign lenders, at least in the foreseeable future. Some established incumbents on Wall Street were critical of the lending frenzy. In August 1929, John Pierpont Morgan Jr wrote to a business partner: 'From what I see of the Germans they are a second-rate people and would rather have their business done for them by someone else.' But for most investors the temptation to invest in the German market was much stronger than the fear of losing money. Also, Allied governments endorsed this lending, seeing it as a way of stabilizing the weak Weimar Republic.[13]

Lending to Germany continued even after the US Federal Reserve began to raise the official interest rate in early 1928 to cool the stock market boom. Long-term capital inflows from the USA abruptly ended in the autumn of 1928, but those streaming in from other countries compensated for this loss. In fact, 1928 was a record year in terms of gross capital imports. And even in 1929, when the Federal Reserve raised the official interest rate again, there was no sudden halt. Short-term capital continued to pour into Germany (Fig. 1.2). This was certainly not sustainable, but the idea that Germany was cut off from foreign funds as a result of high US interest rates is a myth. When Somary addressed his audience in Heidelberg in early 1930, Germany was still receiving foreign short-term funds.[14]

Somary was not the only contemporary who criticized the debt merry-go-round (Illustration 2). Sir Frederick Leith-Ross, a senior British Treasury official, gave a similar warning as early as 1927. 'I remember telling a group of eminent bankers in the City in 1927 that the German banks were too illiquid and that they should restrict their lendings, but my views were treated as unduly alarmist.' Parker Gilbert, the young and forceful American who acted as Agent General for Reparations to Germany in Berlin, repeatedly

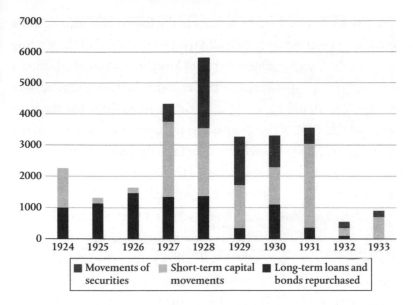

Fig. 1.2 Main components of gross capital flows to Germany (in millions of US dollars)

warned the creditor governments. 'Under present conditions,' he wrote in February 1928 to the Reparation Commission, 'Germany lacks the normal incentive to economize. On the contrary . . . the tendency of recent years has been toward the growth of public expenditures and of public borrowings, both domestic and foreign.'[15]

Hjalmar Schacht, President of the Reichsbank, was a persistent critic of short-term capital movements from the United States to Germany. He told an enquiry commission in October 1926: 'What is actually happening today? Foreign private banks and bankers shower us with gold. They cannot bring enough of it into Germany. The consequence is that foreign governments by the way of the Agent General for Reparations take this gold back to their countries. They relieve us of it, and the question as to how the private

Illustration 2. Cartoon by David Low: 'A reparations sorry-go-round', *Evening Standard*, 29 April 1929: 'Financial Expert: You must pay up the reparations / German Govt.: You must export more goods / German Industry: You must work harder for less wages / German Worker: I must eat up your job / British Worker: You must get me a job / British Industry: You must relieve me of taxation'.

investor, the contributor of capital, will fare, whether he will eventually receive his interest payments and his capital, is left to God.'[16]

Given that Somary's precise prediction was based on sound economic insights shared by other eminent analysts, the question arises as to why policymakers were not able to stabilize Germany's situation before it dragged down the whole world economy. Eighteen months passed between Somary's talk in Heidelberg and the escalation of the German crisis in July 1931. That should have been enough time to forge an international deal, especially between France and Germany.

One answer can be found in the sceptical reactions of Somary's audience in Heidelberg. They simply did not accept the premises on which he based his pessimistic outlook. The chief economics editor at the *Frankfurter Zeitung* responded: 'I very much doubt that we are in a crisis.' Somary received the same reaction when a few days later he presented his view to a prestigious circle that gathered in the noble Hotel Kaiserhof in Berlin. The chief financial officer of Siemens, Max Haller, and the distinguished economics professor Werner Sombart, were not convinced: 'We should not overestimate the influence of the New York stock exchange on the current crisis.' The Siemens official added: 'The loss of one investor is the profit of the other. Stock market quotations are irrelevant for the real economy.' And several German industrialists were convinced that the New York stock exchange crisis would soon be resolved by industrial restructuring and public policies. Somary was adamant, 'I regret having a diametrically opposed view on all points.' Nevertheless, they were not convinced.[17]

Somary's listeners in Berlin and Heidelberg were not the only contemporaries who failed to see the gathering storm. On 29 October 1929, a few days after the crash on Wall Street, the French newspaper *Le Figaro* wrote: 'Our market is comforted by the crisis in New York. Now that the abscess on Wall Street has burst open and the Northern and Central European markets have gotten rid of the excess paper in their possession, we can contemplate a future in brighter colours.' Pierre de Margerie, the French ambassador in Berlin, firmly believed in early February 1930 that the German economy was basically healthy. De Margerie was the son of a philosopher and married to Jeanne Rostand, the sister of the writer Edmond Rostand, who created Cyrano de Bergerac. Not surprisingly, the cultivated French ambassador was more interested in advancing the arts than studying the imbalances of the international economy.[18]

Yet, even an eminent economist like John Maynard Keynes, who was to become one of the most precise analysts of the Great Depression, underestimated the crisis in late 1929 and lost a large amount of his own fortune as a result. One day after the stock market crash, he wrote in the *New York Evening Post*: 'I may be a bad prophet in speaking this way. But I am sure that I am reflecting the instinctive reaction of English financial opinion to the immediate situation. There will be no serious direct consequences in London resulting from the Wall Street slump except to the limited number of Anglo-American securities which are actively dealt in both here and in New York. On the other hand, we find the longer look ahead decidedly encouraging.' Keynes believed that the end of the stock market boom would bring a substantial reduction in interest rates, thus providing a boost to business. 'After cheap money has arrived, a few months have to elapse before the business decisions to which it gives rise can materialise in new trade and industrial activity. But if cheap money does come, I do not doubt its remedial efficacy.'[19]

Somary was not surprised that Keynes underestimated the looming crisis. In June 1926, at a reception held by the German banker Carl Melchior in Berlin, he had talked to him. Asked by Keynes what he was advising his clients, Somary gave the usual pessimistic answer: 'To insulate themselves as much as possible from the coming crisis, and to avoid the markets.' Keynes strongly disagreed. 'We will not have any more crashes in our time. I think the market is very appealing, and prices are low. And where is the crash coming from in any case?' Somary replied: 'The crash will come from the gap between appearance and reality. I have never seen such a storm gathering.' Keynes was not convinced and insisted on talking about shares of individual companies.[20]

Somary's analytical and prognostic capabilities were highly appreciated, but his predictions were ignored. His audience liked his independent thinking, but were confused by his lack of orthodoxy. Somary was often saddened by this state of affairs: 'at the time, I was completely isolated, and my urgent warnings to governments as well as to the business world were universally held against me... I did not expect, nor did I receive, any support for my views from economists. Only a few individuals saw the approaching crisis; wherever I looked, I found only misunderstanding or hostility.'[21]

At a bankers' gathering held in Berlin in the summer of 1929, Charles E. Mitchell, the President of National City Bank, derided Somary as 'the raven of Zurich' who predicted the worst, but kept being wrong and thus having bad luck.[22] People were laughing at the lonely raven.

2

A TRIUMPH OF DIPLOMACY

In January 1930, as Somary was touring through Germany, the tranquil Dutch capital, The Hague, suddenly turned into a hive of activity, welcoming heads of state, ministers, and senior officials from all parts of Europe and Japan. Their task was to conclude the negotiations started at the First Hague Conference in August 1929 and to agree on a final settlement of all the issues that had not been resolved since the end of the war. Most diplomats displayed confidence when asked by the press whether the conference would succeed or not. There was a general sense that, however difficult the situation was, international conflicts should and could be dealt with by conferences and negotiations. On 20 January 1930, in late afternoon, 500 delegates and experts from nearly twenty countries signed the final protocol and the various annexes. It took almost an hour to get all the orange-ribbon-bound documents from one delegation to the other to be signed. The signing was accompanied by a military brass band playing solemn tunes outside the windows where the ceremony took place. The atmosphere was sober, as most delegates were exhausted from the long hours of negotiations and some French ministers had already left for the Naval Conference in London. Nevertheless, everyone present in the venerable Gothic building of the Dutch parliament, the Binnenhof, felt they were witnessing a historic moment.[1]

After the signing ceremony, the chairman of the conference, the Belgian Prime Minister, Henri Jaspar, picked up a gavel, rapped it on the table, and called on Philip Snowden, the British Chancellor of the Exchequer, to speak on behalf of the assembled delegates. He was an odd choice. Despised for his sarcastic criticism of the French and German delegations, Snowden did not have a reputation as a cheerleader. Yet even he was so deeply moved by what had been achieved in The Hague that he could not help expressing a great sense of optimism. Without hesitation, he declared that '[t]he financial problems have been, as we believe, permanently settled, and we shall no longer in this connection be allies and enemies, but we shall all be friends and comrades working together in what remains to be done to complete the pacification of Europe.' In his concluding speech, Chairman Jaspar echoed Snowden's comments and hailed the diplomacy of gradual progress. 'For ten years, the financial problems resulting from the war have been the subject of innumerable international conferences. At each conference one stage further has been reached, and we believe that we have, in the documents we have just signed, brought to a conclusion these long discussions.' His words were received with loud applause.[2]

The next morning, the liberal British press praised the Second Hague Conference wholeheartedly. *The Times* in London wrote that 'a long and difficult chapter in the history of the War was definitively closed'. *The Economist* praised the 'success in The Hague', claiming that 'the past, like a shoddy company whose accounts are in disorder, has at last been liquidated'. On the other side of the Atlantic, the *New York Times* shared this confident view: 'The festering sore has now been healed. The debates and recriminations are over. The problem has been disposed of.'[3]

The French press was less enthusiastic, as Paris had been forced to compromise on several issues. Nevertheless, even the French newspaper *Le Temps*, the unofficial mouthpiece of the French government, strongly endorsed what had been achieved in the Dutch capital: 'The agreements of The Hague mark an important moral and political advance for the whole international situation.'[4] In a similar vein, the pro-government press in Germany reacted positively, although Berlin had not achieved all it wanted either.

The diplomats and politicians gathered in The Hague were particularly proud, because they had succeeded in overcoming the paralysis created by the early death of the German Foreign Minister, Gustav Stresemann, in October 1929. At the First Hague Conference in August 1929, Stresemann had been very ill. In the midst of a conversation with German and French ministers at 1:30 a.m., his hand all of a sudden went to his chest, and he exclaimed: 'I can't anymore!' The German Finance Minister, Rudolf Hilferding, a trained medical doctor, brought him to the Oranje-Hotel where the German delegation was accommodated. When Hilferding returned to inform his colleagues, he explained: 'The clock has run down.' Six weeks later the 51-year-old Stresemann died of a stroke. The *Vossische Zeitung* headlined: 'More than a loss: a calamity!'[5]

Stresemann had single-handedly shaped German foreign policy since 1923. And together with the French Foreign Minister, Aristide Briand, he had done much to improve Franco-German relations. In 1926, they both received the Nobel Peace Prize for concluding the Locarno Treaties (1925) that paved the way for Germany's membership of the League of Nations. When Briand heard of Stresemann's death, he said to his staff that two coffins should be prepared, one for Stresemann and one for himself. 'It's over, everything!' A senior

German official who was in Paris at the time observed when he visited the German embassy in the Rue de Lille: 'In front of the old Palais of the Prince Beauharnais a huge Reich's flag at half-mast was drooping. Briand was leaving the house where he had offered his condolences to the German officials. One could see that he had wept. He knew that with Stresemann's death his own life's work was also being carried to its grave.'[6]

Of course, their relationship had not been free of friction or disappointment, as France and Germany pursued different agendas. For France, the overarching concern was security vis-à-vis Germany, and all measures taken in the field of military, foreign, or financial policy were aimed at making the nation safe from her recent enemy. Germany, in contrast, wanted a revision of the Versailles Treaty and the restoration of pre-war conditions; first and foremost an early evacuation of the occupied Rhineland and the Saar, ultimately the restoration of her pre-war eastern border and the cancellation of reparations. Stresemann's strategy was to achieve the evacuation by negotiating with France, as he understood Briand's security concerns. But still, his was a revisionist agenda. The goal was to regain full sovereignty and to restore Germany's hegemony on continental Europe. In the mid-1920s Germany had a population of 63 million, France only 40 million.[7]

Nevertheless, Briand and Stresemann found a way to engender mutual trust and to loosen the post-war tensions. One reason they understood each other so well was that they had a similar social background. Briand's parents owned a small café on the waterfront in Nantes, the capital of Brittany. Stresemann's parents ran a pub in Berlin and were active in the bottled beer trade. Stresemann would later write a dissertation about this topic which was ridiculed by the radical right. When the two met to discuss politics, they always drank and smoked together: Briand enjoyed wine and cigarettes, Stresemann preferred beer and cigars.[8]

Initially, it seemed as though it would be impossible to overcome the shock of Stresemann's death. His successor, Julius Curtius, a former lawyer and son of an entrepreneur who owned and ran two chemical plants, was not respected by many diplomats. Even some members of his own staff had doubts. Ernst von Weizsäcker, a senior Foreign Ministry official, wrote that Curtius 'had no attractiveness, did not radiate friendship, no "sex-appeal"'. And Briand did not like him at all. The French journalist Geneviève Tabouis, a confidante of Briand, described him as: 'A little lawyer, a little man, correct and meticulous, neither stupid nor intelligent.'[9]

Yet, Curtius, a hard worker who saw himself as 'the executor of Stresemann's testament', proved to be an able chief negotiator. And the arrival of a new French Prime Minister, André Tardieu, helped to renew Franco-German cooperation. Tardieu, who was fourteen years younger than Briand—the same age as Curtius—wanted to open up new lines of communication that were not controlled by his Foreign Minister. Tardieu and Briand were quite different characters. While the latter was not particularly concerned about his appearance, Tardieu had a perfect parting and a trimmed moustache, wore a pince-nez, and used a long, silver cigarette holder when smoking. Like Curtius, he was a child of a good family, a 'gosse des riches'. He had entered the diplomatic service after coming top of his class in the final examinations and then built up a reputation as a conservative commentator, whereas Briand had had to climb the political ladder from the very bottom. During the war, Tardieu had served as press officer on the staff of General Joseph Joffre, then on the staff of General Ferdinand Foch, before becoming commander of an infantry company. Wounded in 1916, he turned his attention to cooperation with the Americans. He worked closely with Prime Minister Georges Clemenceau, who would demand a hard line towards the Germans during the peace negotiations in Paris in 1918–19.[10]

Yet despite appearances, Tardieu and Briand shared the same foreign policy goals, as Tardieu had reinvented himself as a moderate over the course of the 1920s. In 1928, he entered the cabinet of Raymond Poincaré, the dominant figure in French politics at the time, and became the leader of the centre-right faction after Poincaré retired a year later. In November 1929, in the midst of the First Hague Conference, Tardieu became Prime Minister and, seeing that Briand was exhausted, claimed the leading role in French foreign policy.[11]

Illustration 3. French Foreign Minister Aristide Briand (left), Prime Minster André Tardieu (centre), and Finance Minister Henri Chéron (right) in Paris, before departing to the Second Hague Conference, January 1930.

Seeking to build a closer relationship with Curtius, Tardieu invited the German delegation to a breakfast on Saturday morning, two days before the official negotiations were due to restart. The French Prime Minister sat between Curtius and the German Finance Minister Paul Moldenhauer (Illustrations 3 and 4). Over the course of their conversation, they discovered to their great surprise that they had all studied in Bonn in 1897. This was a good ice-breaker. The German public, however, reacted negatively to the event. A photographer, Dr Erich Salomon, managed to take a picture of the breakfast that was published by the *Berliner Illustrirte Zeitung*, implying that Tardieu twisted the German delegation around his finger by offering croissants, coffee, and champagne. Salomon continued to look for ways to get behind the scenes.

Illustration 4. German Foreign Minister Julius Curtius (centre-left) and Finance Minister Paul Moldenhauer (centre-right, with glasses) in Berlin, before departing to the Second Hague Conference, January 1930.

In this, he showed great skills, as a British official recalled: 'One amusing sidelight of the Conference was the success of a German photographer in evading the security restrictions at the various hotels by means of various disguises—including that of an electrician working on the overhead wires—and obtaining some very amusing photographs of Ministers, fast asleep during some prolonged discussions.'[12]

Although the first encounter succeeded in establishing some mutual trust between Tardieu and Curtius, it took nearly three weeks for France, Great Britain, and Germany to strike a deal that would open the way for an understanding with the Eastern and Central European countries. In the final phase, the delegations negotiated day and night, sometimes without interruption. It felt like an endurance race.[13]

At the end of the day, the pressure to save face and the desire to bring a long negotiating process to a successful conclusion prevailed. Whenever the conference threatened to get out of hand, both sides compromised. Most importantly, the British and French representatives gradually accepted Curtius as the legitimate successor of Stresemann. In his speech at the end of the conference, Snowden praised 'the way in which the German delegates, with tenacity, with courage, and yet with the completest courtesy, had defended the interests of their own country'. The French delegation appreciated 'the fairness, the dexterity, and the "national attitude" of the German ministers in the best sense of that phrase'. Despite Stresemann's death and Briand's gradual retreat, international diplomacy continued to function properly.[14]

The centrepiece of the agreements signed in The Hague was the Young Plan—named after the American lawyer and industrialist

Owen Young, who had chaired the preparatory experts' committee meetings in Paris between February and June 1929. The 100-page agreement consisted of fifteen articles and twelve annexes. It redefined the terms of Germany's reparation payments and was thought to be a 'complete and final settlement', as the document asserted.

The reason why European diplomats were still having to deal with German reparations more than ten years after the war was an open secret. Earlier agreements had simply failed to resolve the issue. The Treaty of Versailles of 1919 had stipulated that Germany alone was responsible for the war and therefore had 'to make compensation for all damage done to the civilian population of the Allied and Associated Powers and to their property during the period of the belligerency'. But it did not fix the final bill, thereby opening the way for bitter arguments between the former combatants.[15]

The London Ultimatum of May 1921 was supposed to resolve the issue, but only made things more complicated by fixing the final bill at the extremely high level of 132 billion gold marks—corresponding to roughly 250 per cent of Germany's 1913 GNP. There were three tranches. The A tranche, worth 12 billion gold marks, covered the war damages directly inflicted on the Allies, and the B tranche, amounting to 38 billion gold marks, was thought to finance the war debts France and Great Britain owed to the United States. The C tranche (82 billion gold marks) had only a vague justification, and the negotiators all knew that it was to appease the domestic electorates in the victorious countries and would probably never be paid.

Nevertheless, the 50 billion gold marks in the A and B tranches amounted to almost 100 per cent of Germany's GNP in 1913. The sum could have been substantially lower if the US government had been prepared to reduce its claims on France and Great Britain. But this was taboo in Washington, and the USA was not yet ready to lead and bear the costs of international stability. Accordingly, France and Great Britain simply passed this bill over to Germany. If reparations had only consisted of the direct war damages (the A tranche), they would have been nearly as low as the ones that France had been forced to pay to the German Empire after the lost war of 1870–1, which was around 20 per cent of French GNP in 1871.[16]

Economically, Germany could have paid the reparations, but politically, such a scenario was simply unenforceable, as most German citizens were convinced that their country had not lost the war. Thus, when the cost of the reparation bill became known in Germany, a sort of tax boycott ensued. Taxpayers deferred the submission of their returns until the very last moment, and the authorities delayed demands for arrears, aiming to obstruct the transfer of reparations. The gap between tax receipts and government expenditures was covered by banknotes printed by the central bank which accelerated inflation. The German government transferred only the first cash tranche required by the London Ultimatum, but then virtually stopped paying cash. It also regularly reneged on deliveries in kind, provoking the Belgian and French governments to send troops to the Ruhr region, Germany's western mining district, in January 1923, to collect owed coal (Map 2). Predictably, German workers responded with passive resistance and, to support their struggle, the German government induced the central bank to pay their wages by printing money. As the additional money entered the economy directly via private consumption, the inflation rate, which was already high because of the war and the reconstruction period, accelerated and eventually led to full-blown hyperinflation.[17]

Germany's public order was on the brink of collapse. Even the Austrian writer Stefan Zweig who had experienced hyperinflation in Vienna in 1921–2 was overwhelmed by the chaos in Germany: 'The mark plunged, never to stop until it had reached the fantastic figures of madness—the millions, the billions and trillions. Now the real witches' sabbath of inflation started, ... I have known days when I had to pay fifty thousand marks for a newspaper in the morning and a hundred thousand in the evening; whoever had foreign currency to exchange did so from hour to hour, because at four o'clock he would get a better rate than at three, and at five o'clock he would get much more than he had got an hour earlier.'[18]

The effects of hyperinflation were brutal and unevenly distributed. Anyone having savings and holding bonds lost their wealth. Real wages as well as welfare payments declined as the inflation rate surpassed the pace at which nominal wages and rents were being adjusted to rising prices. On the other hand, those citizens, companies, and bodies that were in debt profited from hyperinflation, as their liabilities denominated in German currency were annihilated. Most importantly, German governments—the Reich, the states (called Länder), and the communes—saw their debts denominated in German currency disappear. This was detrimental for creditors, both domestic and foreign, but advantageous for the German taxpayer.

All these sudden upheavals had a demoralizing effect on the vast majority of the German population. Many voters, especially the middle classes who had lost their savings, were traumatized and disillusioned with the young Weimar Republic.[19]

In late 1923, the German government, afraid of losing control, withdrew its policy of passive resistance. The following year, the Allies also made a step forward, engaging Charles Dawes, an American lawyer, politician, and brigadier-general, to chair an experts' committee to make proposals for rescheduling German reparations. (One year later, Dawes would receive the Nobel Peace Prize and become Vice President of the United States under President Calvin Coolidge.) The Dawes Plan brought several improvements for Germany. First, it lowered the annual repayment instalments and provided the Reich with a foreign loan, the so-called Dawes International Loan, to enable a smooth transition to the new payment schedule. Second a new currency, the Reichsmark, backed by gold, was introduced to establish monetary stability. And finally, Belgium and France withdrew their troops from the Ruhr region. In return, Germany had to accept a certain level of foreign control. The Reichsbank and the Reichsbahn were made independent of the government and supervised by foreign experts, and an Agent General for Reparation Payments was installed in Berlin to control the flow of repayments.

On the surface, the Dawes Plan worked remarkably well. The Dawes International Loan, underwritten by the leading American bank J. P. Morgan, was oversubscribed ten times in New York. Spurred by this outburst of confidence, the German economy recovered quickly. Between 1923 and 1927, industrial production more than doubled. Germany's economic renaissance also stimulated the world economy. The Dow Jones index, after a disappointing performance in 1923, entered an extended boom period, and American lending to Europe and Latin America soon reached record high levels, with Germany the most important recipient. The restoration of the gold standard and the independent status

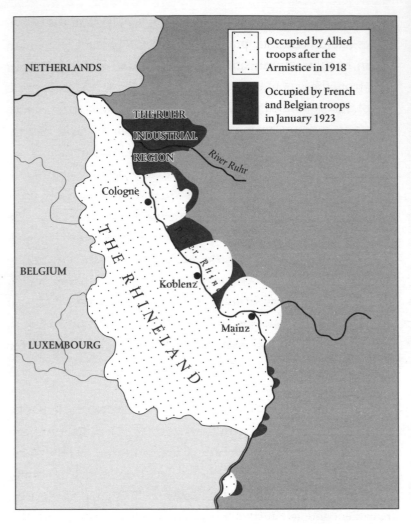

Map 2. The occupation of the Ruhr Valley and the Rhineland

of the Reichsbank supervised by the Allies guaranteed exchange rate stability and capital mobility. Even better, investments in Germany offered higher interest rates than the US bond market because German hunger for capital was enormous following the ravages of hyperinflation. And as mentioned, hyperinflation also had the positive effect that the Reich, the Länder, and the communes had no domestic public debt anymore. France and Great Britain, by contrast, were sitting on huge domestic debt piles stemming from the war. In 1920, they amounted to more than 100 per cent of their combined 1913 GNP. Thus, Germany was an Eldorado for foreign investors, mainly from the United States, but also from Great Britain, the Netherlands, Sweden, and Switzerland.[20]

Yet, as all parties involved in the negotiations knew, the reparations issue remained unresolved. 'The Dawes Plan was only a provisional settlement of the German debt', a member of the British delegation recalled. The priority of the Dawes Plan was to end diplomatic tensions between France and Germany and to restore confidence in Germany's currency and public finances after the disaster of hyperinflation. However, the basic defects of the reparation scheme were not addressed. The parameters had been set in 1919, and as diplomacy is highly path-dependent, only gradual changes were possible.[21]

Two weaknesses of the Dawes Plan were particularly obvious. First, it only defined the annual repayment schedule. In the short term, this proved to be useful to restart the whole process, but in the medium term it undermined the credibility of the whole framework. The three tranches fixed by the London Ultimatum of 1921 were neither removed from the table nor were they confirmed. Second, as time went by, it became increasingly difficult to maintain the foreign supervision of Germany's public finances.

Even more alarming was that the Dawes Plan helped create international imbalances which, from the perspective of critical observers, such as Felix Somary, had the potential to unravel the whole European financial and monetary system. The cause for concern was the way the so-called transfer protection clause operated. According to the Dawes Plan, it was designed to help the Reich by giving it the freedom to delay annual payments if they threatened the stability of the currency. In reality, however, as foreign bankers and investors rapidly understood, transfer protection meant that the claims of private creditors had priority over reparations because the latter could always be delayed. Thus, the Dawes Plan made lending to Germany even more attractive than it already was.[22]

As a result, Germany was able to borrow vast amounts of foreign capital which only partially served to make productive investments. A large share was also used to extend public services to record high levels. Accordingly, Germany's foreign debt denominated in foreign gold-based currencies—and being to a considerable degree short-term—increased rapidly. In 1929, the Reich had foreign debts amounting to RM 89 billion corresponding to roughly 75 per cent of GDP. And as a large portion of this foreign capital inflow was channelled through the financial system, the capital ratios of the large commercial banks had dropped dramatically. For this reason, Somary considered the German banking system to be the 'weakest link where the collapse will and must occur'.[23]

The Young Plan of 1930 tried to end these dangerous developments by improving Germany's position in three respects. First, it reduced the yearly payment from RM 2.5 billion to roughly RM 2 billion, which corresponded to about 3 per cent of the German economy in 1930. Second, Germany was liberated from foreign financial control. The Reparation Commission was dissolved, and the job of Parker Gilbert, the Agent General for Reparations, ended. Now, Berlin was back in charge of transfers of reparations, with the newly founded Bank for International Settlements (BIS) in Basle serving as a trust office. The Young Plan also ended the Allies' oversight of the Reichsbahn and the Reichsbank. Third, the Allies guaranteed that they would withdraw their troops from the Rhineland five years earlier than stipulated in the Versailles Treaty (Map 2). The new date was 30 June 1930. This clause was not written in the Young Plan itself, but it was the precondition for Germany's consent.[24]

On the other hand, there were two major disadvantages for Germany in the Young Plan. First, the Reich had to pay reparations until 1988, i.e. over a period of fifty-eight years. Such a long duration was rather odd. Even Owen Young, the architect of the plan, acknowledged during the negotiations that 'no practical man would want to assess the solvency of a country for more than fifteen years'. Moreover, it was politically counterproductive, as it gave the opponents of the Young Plan the argument that Germans would be in debt for three generations. Also, the Young Plan changed the transfer protection clause. Henceforth, Germany would be obliged to pay at least RM 612 million per year, no matter what. This tranche was called the unconditional annuity. The payment of the rest—roughly RM 1.3 billion—could be delayed for two years if the German government wished a temporary suspension, for example due to a recession. At first glance, this looked like a minor technical revision. But it was much more than that. It effectively reversed the ranking of Germany's foreign debts. From now on, reparation payments came first, servicing private foreign debts second. Borrowing from abroad suddenly became more difficult because foreign banks and investors feared that their claims would not be honoured in times of crisis. This in turn curtailed the leeway of policymakers in Berlin. The Reich now had to run a budget and a trade surplus to be able to pay reparations. And as the German economy had entered a recession in 1929, this new policy requirement was likely to worsen the slump. In order to achieve budget and trade surpluses, there would have to be budget cuts, higher taxes, and lower wages and prices. Needless to say, reducing domestic demand in a time of crisis was politically counterproductive, especially in a precarious democracy like the Weimar Republic.[25]

Some Germans immediately recognized the negative consequences of this new clause introduced by the Young Plan. Among them were Hjalmar Schacht, the President of the Reichsbank, and Albert Vögler, a leading steel industry executive, both of whom had represented Germany on the Young committee in Paris (Illustration 5). The reversal of debt seniority was one of the reasons Schacht stepped down from the Reichsbank in March

Illustration 5. Young Plan conference chaired by Owen Young (at the end of the table) at Hotel George V in Paris, 1929.

of 1930. Vögler thought the new seniority rule was a sufficient reason to reject the Young Plan and departed from Paris before the negotiations were concluded. Yet, the new clause remained. Schacht enjoyed little credibility in government circles, since his opposition to the Young Plan had almost shipwrecked the Second Hague Conference. Vögler too had lost standing since he left the German People's Party (DVP) in 1924 in disgust about the 'policy of fulfilment' pursued by Stresemann.[26]

More important, senior German government officials and politicians were convinced that a failure of the Young Plan would trigger a financial crisis, and they were counting on positive economic effects from the diplomatic breakthrough in The Hague. Finance Minister Paul Moldenhauer was confident that after the government won the battle in the Reichstag Germany's political tensions would dissipate and business would be stimulated. Hans Schäffer, his influential State Secretary at the German Finance Ministry who was close to the left-wing liberal German Democratic Party and the Social Democrats, shared this optimism. He believed that the Young Plan would bring about a strong revival of the world economy—just as the Dawes Plan had done six years earlier. Similarly, Jacob Goldschmidt, head of the Darmstädter und Nationalbank (Danat Bank), one of the largest commercial banks of Germany, and Max Warburg, a highly respected partner of the merchant bank M. M. Warburg & Co. in Hamburg, predicted a strong rise in international lending. Even Carl Melchior, another partner of M. M. Warburg & Co., who had been involved in many post-war conferences and was known for his prudent judgement, was guardedly optimistic.[27]

In contrast, Felix Somary remained deeply pessimistic. When hearing of the new scheme, he said: 'Ave Caesar, *moratoria* te

salutant!' For Somary, it was obvious that diplomats and politicians were suffering collectively from a lack of economic literacy: 'The materialist conception of history embodied in Marxist
thought has overestimated the importance of economic factors in the political life of nations; but bourgeois statesmen and
diplomats, to the vast detriment of their peoples, have grossly
underestimated it. How often have leading diplomats considered
knowledge of economic matters unnecessary and taken pride in
their own ignorance!'

Instead, he complained, they invested too much in new institutions such as the BIS. 'There is a remarkable tendency in our time:
when we require some ideas to solve a problem, we establish an
organization instead. The organization is of no practical help, in
fact it increases the confusion, does not do what it should, creates
a growing bureaucracy that then becomes an end in itself; and
finally goes on existing long after the entire world has forgotten
when and why the organization was ever established.'

Somary could hardly believe the contrast between the long
schedule of German reparations and the precariously short-term
horizon of Germany's debts: 'Almost all the great powers have been
negotiating for months about how many billions a year should be
paid until 1966, and thereafter until 1988, by a country that is not
even in a position to pay its own civil servants' salaries.'[28] Somary
knew from his own experience how precarious the financial situation of the Reich had become. In the spring of 1929, Germany
had faced a sudden currency crisis because the press had reported
that the Young Plan negotiations in Paris threatened to break
down completely. On 25 April, the Reichsbank was confronted
with a dramatic drain of reserves and raised the official interest
rate to 7.5 per cent, while commercial banks were threatened by

serious liquidity shortages. The Reichsbank came under such strong pressure that it refused to accept the treasury bills of the Reich. The situation threatened to slide out of control. Finance Minister Rudolf Hilferding, a Social Democrat, became increasingly desperate. The 52-year-old Hilferding had become famous for his theoretical book *Financial Capital* (1910) in which he predicted an increasing dominance of the financial sector over the economy, eventually leading to monopolistic capitalism. Now he was seeking any financial capital he could get his hands on to end the crisis.

At the beginning of May, Hilferding proposed floating a tax-free long-term bond, but there was strong resistance both within the cabinet and in parliament. In mid-May, exasperated from lengthy negotiations, Hilferding called Somary, a long-time friend from his student days. He needed 100 million Swiss francs in order to pay the salaries of the civil servants. There was a sense of despair, as Somary recalled: 'In the name of the entire German government, Hilferding begged me urgently for help, saying that there was nobody else to whom he could turn.' It was a large sum, essential to bridge the funding shortage.

Somary felt obliged to help his friend and immediately informed the Swiss National Bank. Two days later a consortium was formed under the leadership of Somary's bank, Blankart & Cie., and including the leading Swiss insurance companies, putting a short-term loan of 50 million Swiss francs at the disposal of the Reich. At the request of Hilferding, Somary then flew to Paris where Schacht was participating in a meeting of the Young committee. The deal was done, and the German government received the money just in time. Later when the currency crisis abated, Hilferding promptly paid the loan back.[29]

In his sceptical view of the Second Hague Conference, Somary would ultimately prove to have been right. The Young Plan was a scheme based on a benign scenario that was unrealistic. A financial storm was gathering, but, unfortunately, diplomats and politicians were ignoring the warning signs. In January 1930, when meeting in the Dutch capital, they still lacked a sense of urgency.

3

'STRONG CARDS TO PLAY'

On 12 March 1930, nearly two months after the Second Hague Conference, the Reichstag, the first chamber of the German parliament, passed the Young Plan with a clear majority. The Länder, assembled in the Reichsrat, favoured the Young Plan with an even higher margin.[1] The *Vossische Zeitung*, a pillar of the pro-Weimar press, reacted with great relief: 'A new stage of pacification is achieved.'[2]

It was not an easy victory, however. The ruling Grand Coalition under Chancellor Hermann Müller had been under enormous pressure from radical political forces. On the day of the final parliamentary debate a large crowd gathered in the zone between the Brandenburg Gate and the Reichstag. The galleries in the chamber were filled with spectators, and almost all deputies were present—a rare event. At noon, the President of the Reichstag opened the session and called Chancellor Müller to the speaker's desk. The 54-year-old bespectacled Social Democrat looked tired, exhausted from the negotiations, and afflicted by a severe illness.[3]

Müller had hardly begun to speak when he was interrupted by deputies of the radical Right and the radical Left. He carried on, but at one point, Joseph Goebbels, the head of the Berlin district of the National Socialist German Workers' Party (NSDAP), was shouting so aggressively that the President of the Reichstag had to intervene: 'Deputy Goebbels, I call you to order and ask you not to continue making interjections.' Nevertheless, the Chancellor's speech continued to provoke shouts, laughter, and all sorts of noise. The situation got completely out of hand when a deputy of the National Socialists in his speech accused the government of 'treason against the people'. When Müller finished, the whole Reichstag was in uproar. An enraged deputy of the German Democratic Party shouted: 'That such a lout is allowed to speak!'[4]

What made the opposition of the radical Right so visceral was not only the Young Plan, but also its link to a German–Polish agreement stipulating that Germany and Poland renounced all financial claims, both public and private, stemming from the world war and the Versailles Treaty. A deputy of the German National People's Party (DNVP), the largest parliamentary group of the radical Right, explained: 'Up there in room 12, there hangs a map of the German East, how it was and how it is. This map has a shocking effect on anybody looking at it attentively, and I wish this map were widely distributed and hung up in every classroom.'[5]

The Right had been mobilizing against the Young Plan since June 1929 when the Experts' Committee had released a draft. The chairman of the DNVP, Alfred Hugenberg, a former executive at Friedrich Krupp AG, business lobbyist and owner of a media conglomerate including the film production company UFA, founded the 'Reich Committee for the German People's Petition Against the Young Plan and the War-Guilt Lie'. At the end of September, the committee submitted a draft bill to be put to referendum. It renounced the recognition of 'war-guilt' (Article 231 of the Versailles Treaty), opposed new reparations, and made it a criminal offence for the chancellor, ministers, and government officials to sign any reparation agreement with foreign powers. Ultimately, the referendum on 22 December failed: only 15 per cent of German voters went to the polls, well below the 50 per cent required for a referendum to pass. But nearly 95 per cent of the votes case were in favour of the bill, giving the radical Right 'ownership' of popular resentment against Versailles and the Young Plan.

One figure profited enormously from the campaign against the Young Plan: Adolf Hitler, the 'Führer' of the Nazi Party. Before the vote, hardly anybody outside of the radical Right took notice of this hysterical politician with the comedic moustache and the strident voice. The NSDAP had won only 2.6 per cent of the vote in the 1928 Reichstag elections—0.4 percentage points less than in the 1924 elections. Yet, as he became part of the inner circle of Hugenberg's Reich Committee, he gained access to influential circles and was featured regularly on Hugenberg's powerful media outlets. Hitler would soon become a household name (Illustration 6).[6]

On the far Left, the Communists agitated against the Young Plan with the same fervour as the Right, even though the motivation was quite different. As they considered capitalism the root of all evil, reparations were considered yet another manifestation of this dysfunctional system. In the parliamentary debate, one of the Communist deputies explained that the Young Plan 'was supposed to subject the working people of Germany for decades to the double exploitation by German and foreign capital.' He concluded: 'This Young pact is not, as the Social Democrats say, a step to peace, but an imperialistic war pact on the back of, and at the expense of, the working class.'[7]

Chancellor Müller did his best to hold his own against the opposition, but he did not have particularly strong arguments.

Illustration 6. Poster supporting referendum against Young Plan in December 1929: 'Until the third generation you will have to labour'.

He explained that, though far from perfect, the Young Plan would bring an improvement for Germany. 'We consider the new agreement to be an advance relative to the previous state of affairs.' Then, the vote was taken. In theory, the Grand Coalition should have prevailed easily. It held 301 out of 491 seats, consisting of five major parties: the Social Democrats (SPD), the German Democrats (DDP), the Centre Party (Zentrumspartei), the Bavarian People's Party (BVP), and the German People's Party (DVP). In practice, however, quite a few deputies sympathized with the arguments put forward by the opposition. Thus, in the end, only 265 voted yes against 192 no, with three abstentions. The vote on the German–Polish agreement was even closer: 236 yes, 217 no, with eight abstentions. This result marked a success for the radical parties holding only 139 out of a total of 491 seats: 12 by the National Socialists, 73 by the DNVP, and 54 by the Communists. The Grand Coalition prevailed, but it was in no way a convincing victory.[8]

Chancellor Müller's difficulties did not go unnoticed in Paris. Nevertheless, Le Temps, the pro-government newspaper, ended its editorial with a positive note: 'We enter a new era.'[9] The French were particularly relieved that Paul von Hindenburg, President of the German Reich, signed the bill only one day after the parliamentary session. It was no secret that supporting the Young Plan did not come naturally to the massive, 83-year-old imperial field marshal with his walrus moustache and crewcut. Everybody knew that he felt emotionally and politically close to the DNVP and its campaign for the end of reparations and the restoration of the old borders in the east.

Born in 1847 in the city of Posen, 200 km east of Berlin, Hindenburg was typical of the Junker class, the landed nobility of that region (Illustration 7). The family estate was in Neudeck

Illustration 7. President Paul von Hindenburg, 1930.

in the Prussian heartland, about 100 km south of Danzig. He participated in the Franco-Prussian War of 1870/1 and was present in the Hall of Mirrors at Versailles when Wilhelm I was proclaimed Kaiser of the new German Empire. From 1903 to 1911 he was the Commanding General of the 4th Army Corps. His wife was Gertrud von Sperling, the daughter of a nobleman officer, with whom he had three children. And, as a practising Prussian Protestant, he regularly went to church.

Hindenburg's reluctance to sign the Young Plan was not only motivated by his social background. He also feared that his charisma would evaporate if he became too much involved in the struggles between the Social Democrats and the parties he felt close to. Contrary to his outer appearance as the benevolent father of the nation, he was a political animal. His ability to win both institutional power and public admiration had proven to be particularly useful during the First World War. Shortly after the outbreak of war, when Germany was losing ground against the invading Russian army in the East, the then 67-year-old Hindenburg was named general of the 8th Army and, mostly thanks to his able Chief of Staff Erich Ludendorff, won the battle of Tannenberg. Yet it was not Ludendorff who gained laurels, but Hindenburg who made sure that all the praise was showered on himself as the highest military commander of the victorious army. He became a hugely popular war hero and was named General Field Marshal. Bit by bit, he expanded his power, until in August 1916 he assumed together with Ludendorff the leadership of the General Staff (Oberste Heeresleitung OHL), marginalizing the government and the Kaiser in the process.

Although Germany lost the war, Hindenburg succeeded in maintaining his mythical status as the victor of the battle of Tannenberg. He was brought back from retirement in 1925 when the conservative parties were looking for an able candidate for the presidency of the Reich. Thanks to his heroic status, Hindenburg won the election and assumed the highest political office of the Weimar Republic even though he had never embraced the democratic form of government. His victory was a turning point in his life and in the history of the Weimar Republic.

In the first four years of his presidency, Hindenburg had little difficulty in maintaining his superior pose. The political quarrels remained within the realm of the government and did not threaten his duty to be above politics. But with the Young Plan overwhelming domestic politics, he became a target of the nationalist parties who were politically close to him. In October

1929, twenty-two former army generals and navy admirals wrote him a letter to try to persuade him to join their cause. Hindenburg would not budge, but he knew that by supporting the Young Plan he was putting his prestige at risk.[10]

His scepticism grew when in the beginning of March 1930 Hjalmar Schacht resigned from the presidency of the Reichsbank because of the Young Plan. Thus, when the Reichstag in mid-March passed the plan with a clear majority, he issued a public statement after signing the bill in which he made it clear that he was not happy. He also hesitated for several days before signing the German–Polish liquidation agreement, citing constitutional reservations. Eventually he endorsed it, but his hesitation signalled his reluctance to normalize post-war relations with Poland.[11]

Hindenburg's fear of tainting his image as a result of his support for the Young Plan had far-reaching consequences. The Weimar Constitution gave the President significant powers, making him a kind of a surrogate Kaiser, and, increasingly, Hindenburg was willing to use them. He was tired of being attacked for his collaboration with the Left and sought the restoration of a centre-right minority government as had existed from 1925 to 1928. He wanted a cabinet that was only loosely tied to the parliamentary parties and which governed on the basis of presidential prerogatives and, with the help of military allies, developed a plan to achieve his aim.[12]

The mastermind behind the plan was the intelligent and witty, but also secretive and ruthless, Kurt von Schleicher, a major general who headed the powerful Office of Ministerial Affairs in the Defence Ministry and would later become the penultimate Chancellor to Hitler.[13] Schleicher advocated the use of Article 48 of the Weimar Constitution that gave the President the power to sign emergency bills into law without the consent of the Reichstag.

Article 48 had the following wording: 'If public security and order are seriously disturbed or endangered within the German Reich, the President of the Reich may take measures necessary for their restoration, intervening if need be with the assistance of the armed forces.' The Reichstag could cancel any law based on Article 48 by a simple majority within sixty days of its passage but, in return, the President could dissolve the Reichstag.

Of course, using Article 48 was controversial. It was an emergency clause, not a free pass for the political preferences of the President. But there had been an important precedent showing that there was room for a flexible interpretation. In 1923/4, when the German government ended hyperinflation and stabilized the currency, it justified its measures with Article 48, and this procedure was endorsed by the then President, Friedrich Ebert, a Social Democrat. Thus, the use of Article 48 as Hindenburg and Schleicher had in mind was problematic but not entirely unheard of.

Hindenburg and his entourage began to undermine the Grand Coalition and waited for the right moment to act. A golden opportunity came in mid-March of 1930. The fight for the Young Plan had forged a certain unity among the ruling coalition, but once the plan was passed, their division on fiscal issues re-emerged. In relative terms, the fiscal imbalance was not huge. In 1929, the budget deficit amounted to no more than 2 per cent of national income. In the fiscal year of 1928/9, public debt as a percentage of GNP increased by only 4 per cent. But the way it was financed was not sustainable. The Reich was in desperate need of obtaining long-term loans, but increasingly had to resort to foreign short-term funds that needed to be constantly renewed and were subject to volatile price swings, depending on the country's fiscal and political situation. Furthermore, the economy began to stagnate in 1928 and entered a recession in 1929, well before the stock market crash on Wall Street.[14]

One important cause of the budget deficit was the so-called *Extraordinarium*, i.e. inherited spending commitments or promises that had not been properly funded. The other was unemployment insurance losses. According to the 1927 law that introduced a generous insurance scheme, the Reich had to support the Unemployment Insurance Fund once the unemployment rate reached more than 1.4 million. The generosity of the lawmakers was understandable, as it served to enhance the legitimacy of the Weimar Republic. Yet, as the German economy slowed, the number of unemployed jumped well above this threshold. By January 1930, the number of unemployed people registered at Labour Exchanges reached more than 3 million—corresponding to an unemployment rate of approximately 15 per cent. Of course, part of this increase was due to seasonal factors. But relative to January 1928 when the economy was still growing, the number of unemployed people had almost doubled.[15]

So far, the Grand Coalition had always found a way to avoid budget and cabinet crises. But after passing the Young Plan, conflict over the funding of unemployment insurance had the potential to bring down the Müller cabinet. The Social Democrats wanted higher contributions while the German People's Party wanted to cut spending. After several rounds of negotiations, a consensus emerged within the cabinet, but it required that the Social Democrats in the Reichstag make a step towards the centre-right parties. They refused. Chancellor Müller had lost the support of his own party and was forced to resign. Whether or not the fall of the Grand Coalition was inevitable has been often debated by historians: some highlight the accidental course of events, others considered the end of the Müller cabinet inevitable. In any event, the opportunity to get rid of the Social Democrats was welcomed by President Hindenburg.[16]

But removing Müller was not sufficient. The old Field Marshal also needed a politician who understood the nuts and bolts of fiscal policy. And he wished to have a chancellor who could put an end to petty politics, bring the economy back on track, and support the ailing agricultural sector. There was only one candidate in his camp who met these requirements: Heinrich Aloysius Maria Elisabeth Brüning, the parliamentary leader of the Catholic Centre Party.[17]

Brüning's background was very different from Hindenburg's (Illustration 8). He was born in 1885 in the Catholic city of Münster

Illustration 8. Chancellor Heinrich Brüning, 1930.

in Westphalia, a part of Prussia since the end of the Napoleonic wars and therefore a centre of the 'Kulturkampf' between Protestants and Catholics in the late nineteenth century. He was brought up in a typical middle-class family of Wilhelminian Germany. His father had inherited a vinegar factory and built up a flourishing wine dealership. Heinrich studied law as well as history, philosophy, and economics, spending no fewer than eleven years at university. In 1904, he entered the University of Munich, in 1906 he went to Strasbourg, in 1911 to the London School of Economics and Political Science, and finally in 1913 to Bonn to write his dissertation about the financial, economic, and legal situation of English railways.

In 1915, he volunteered for the German infantry, was twice wounded, and became a company commander by the end of the war. For his bravery, he was awarded both the second- and first-class Iron Cross. The war proved a defining experience for him as for many of his generation. Instead of pursuing an academic career he felt the need to contribute to the common good by helping returning soldiers to find jobs. Soon he worked for the Prussian welfare department and was an executive director of the non-socialist Confederation of German Trade Unions (Deutscher Gewerkschaftsbund). In 1924, he was elected to the Reichstag for the Centre Party, becoming its parliamentary leader in 1929. Politically, Brüning reflected all wings of his party. He was a fiscal conservative, but also welcomed the welfare state. He advocated a revision of the Treaty of Versailles, but also endorsed negotiations with the Allies. He regretted that the monarchy had collapsed, but he also defended the Weimar Republic against the radical Left and Right.[18]

Thanks to his war experience as a field officer, he was politically reliable for Hindenburg. And as he had distinguished himself as a leading financial expert in the Reichstag, he seemed able to lead a technocratic government. The only problem was his deep-rooted Catholicism. Hindenburg was reassured that Brüning felt and acted like a 'protestant Catholic', being a relentless worker with high moral standards and an admirer of Prussian virtues. When he decided to make a career as a public servant and politician, he consciously postponed marriage, feeling that 'whoever dedicates himself to service to humanity and the public good should not be devoted to any one person, should not start a family'.[19] The official portrait shows a sober politician with a dour face. He was the perfect embodiment of an austere technocrat, lacking any charisma.[20]

Brüning himself did not actively seek the chancellorship. On the contrary, he tried to preserve the Grand Coalition. At the same time, he did not object to Hindenburg and Schleicher's plan. This ambiguous approach was typical. Brüning had the reputation of a laggard who 'reflected on all decisions in a thorough manner, often too long, inclined to adopt a step-by-step approach', as a senior official of the German Finance Ministry would later recall. He was also highly secretive, always afraid of being surrounded by opponents and plotters who tried to throw him out of office. 'Sometimes his anxiety literally degenerated into paranoia', the same official wrote in his memoirs.[21]

In the end, things took their course, just as Hindenburg and Schleicher had planned. On Thursday evening, 27 March, Müller went to the President to offer his resignation, whereupon Brüning's friend Gottfried Treviranus, who was at a private reception, received a phone call from the President's office as the soup was being served. 'The President wishes to see Dr Brüning tomorrow morning at 9 a.m. regarding the formation of a new government. We cannot reach him. Could you help us find him?' Treviranus went to the 'Rheingold' restaurant near Potsdamer Platz and discovered his friend at his usual table. Brüning hesitated, but eventually agreed to meet the President the next morning and accept the offer to become Chancellor. In the next three days, Brüning formed a cabinet which was sworn in by Hindenburg on Monday, 31 March 1930.[22]

The composition of the cabinet reflected the wishes of the President as never before in the history of the Weimar Republic. Even the *Vossische Zeitung*, a pro-government newspaper, was amazed. Hindenburg insisted on the appointment of two ministers from the nationalist right: Martin Schiele, a member of the DNVP, President of the Reichslandbund (dominated by conservative big landowners) and opponent of the Young Plan, for the Ministry of Agriculture (Reichsernährungsminister), and Treviranus, a defector from the DNVP who in January 1930 had formed a new parliamentary group called the Conservative People's Party. Hindenburg also requested that Brüning keep his friend Georg Schätzel as Reichspostminister. Brüning accepted.[23]

The constitutional significance of the transition from Müller to Brüning cannot be overstated. The collapse of the Grand Coalition marked the end of a normal parliamentary democracy, as the parties represented in Brüning's cabinet did not have a majority in the Reichstag. It was being replaced by a presidential system based on Hindenburg's emergency decrees. The new Chancellor also stood for a more assertive foreign policy. The ultimate goal was to regain the old hegemony in continental Europe. To restore this position, Germany had to break free of reparations, revise the eastern border, and strengthen ties with Austria.[24]

Yet, the political shift should not be exaggerated. The abolition of reparations, the revision of the eastern border, and the cooperation with Austria were goals that were shared by all parties. And in the field of fiscal policy, there was nearly complete continuity, as Germany was condemned to pursue austerity. In addition, the group of ministers and senior officials who were in charge of implementing austerity stayed in office, in particular Finance Minister Moldenhauer and, even more importantly, his State Secretary, Hans Schäffer, who became the crucial figure in economic and fiscal affairs during the Brüning era. Schäffer, a lawyer from Breslau who was close to the left-wing liberal German Democratic Party, had entered the civil service shortly after the war. He was an able mediator and idea generator and was considered to be 'the heart and the mind of the Brüning cabinet', as a senior official recalled. He was notorious for making private stenographic summaries of all meetings, phone calls, and conversations. Thanks to him, we know almost every detail about the unfolding of the German crisis.[25]

The strong emphasis on continuity also reassured markets and investors. The *Vossische Zeitung* headlined on Friday evening, one day after the resignation of Chancellor Müller: 'Cabinet crisis has no effect: positive market sentiment.' In London, there was no panic either. The price of the Dawes Bond hardly moved, and the German currency remained firm. The *Financial Times* wrote that investors 'were relieved by the prospect of a regime less under the domination of socialism'. The same relaxed atmosphere prevailed on Wall Street. The Dow Jones Industrial Average climbed on Friday, 28 March, the day after Müller's resignation, and again on Monday, 31 March, when the new government was sworn in.[26]

In step with the markets, the leading newspapers in Great Britain and the United States were not at all alarmed. The *New York Times* explicitly referred to the continuity in foreign policy:

'Whatever the political changes, it seems certain that the present Foreign Minister, Dr. Curtius, who succeeded Dr. Stresemann, will remain in office. Part of the wisdom of the German leaders has lain in their realization that no matter how acute the internal crises, it is essential to maintain a continuous foreign policy.' The Berlin correspondent of *The Times* reminded his readers of historical precedents: 'Political memories in Germany are short, and the idea of a Government not based on a formal coalition has been treated as something new. But Dr Brüning's Cabinet, if he succeeds in forming one, will hardly differ at all from a "Cabinet of personalities" such as that formed by Herr Müller after the last elections.' Two days later, when the new cabinet was presented, he wrote: 'Dr. Brüning, who has the President's full confidence, has several strong cards to play, and there is no reason so far to take very seriously the suspicion that, in allying himself with the Young Conservatives and the Agrarians, he may, consciously or unconsciously, be lending himself to a subtle Nationalist scheme to bring about a dictatorship.' Likewise, *The Economist* remained cool: 'There is an element of instability here; but probably the difficulty will prove to be greater in theory than in practice.'[27]

The French press was more reserved towards the new German government, but the papers close to the government would not criticize it too severely. *Le Temps* wrote that the Brüning cabinet should be judged according to its deeds and not to rumours. The newspaper *L'Œuvre*, close to Foreign Minister Aristide Briand, was hopeful, considering Brüning 'an expert in financial affairs, the best leader of his party and one of the most respected members of the Reichstag'. *Le Petit Parisien* wrote that the resignation of the Müller cabinet had no significance for foreign policy, but only for domestic fiscal policy. The next day the same newspaper also predicted that the pro-Weimar parties would do everything to avoid a dissolution of the Reichstag, given that elections would only help the Communists and the Radical Right.[28]

The French newspapers belonging to the opposition were more critical. They felt that the German parliamentary system was compromised. The commentary by the right-wing daily *Le Figaro* was particularly negative, predicting that 'the crisis unfolding threatens to be one of the most severe and profound ones that Germany has known for ten years. Even if not all the signs are misleading, we fear that the resignation of the Müller cabinet is only the beginning of a cascade of crises, at more or less long intervals, until we approach radical measures: dissolution of the Reichstag or application of article 48 of the Weimar Constitution. Whatever happens, the parliamentary regime is not about to become stronger in Germany.'[29]

Yet, despite some gloomy editorials, the general mood was still quite positive in London, Paris, New York, and Washington. The new German government seemed to be serious about fiscal restructuring, even though there was some collateral damage done to the Weimar democracy. Many believed that a technocrat like Brüning was in a better position to cope with the financial problems than his Social Democratic predecessor. Furthermore, in the weeks following the inauguration of the new cabinet, good news came from Berlin. On 3 April, Brüning won a vote of no-confidence in the Reichstag, demonstrating that he was capable of governing despite not having a majority. Eleven days later, he convinced the Reichstag to pass the first part of the financial programme which had brought down the Müller cabinet. The plan was passed with a slim majority. Hermann Pünder, Chief of Staff of the Chancellery, wrote in his diary: 'From morning to late evening one vote followed after another. The tension was indescribable, perhaps the worst in the history of the Reichstag.'[30]

Other good news followed. Germany's approval of the Young Plan gave access to the big loan the government had negotiated with the Swedish financier Ivar Kreuger. In exchange for giving Kreuger a monopoly over the match industry, Germany received $125 million. It allowed the government to overcome its short-term funding problems for the rest of the year. As a result, Finance Minister Moldenhauer, in a speech in early May in the Reichstag, felt encouraged to hold out the prospect of a balanced budget for the ongoing fiscal year and a tax cut in the following year.[31]

Elsewhere, there was also reason for optimism. In late March and early April, both chambers of the French parliament passed the Young Plan with a large majority. Moreover, in the first two quarters of 1930 the French economy was still resisting recession, although exports were suffering from weakening global demand. Industrial production remained stable, the unemployment rate was at a historic low.[32] Parisian cafés, cinemas, and night clubs were all thriving.

On 17 May, three other pieces of encouraging news emerged: first, the Young Plan became effective, retroactive to September 1929, and the Bank for International Settlements (BIS) in Basle began to operate; second, the French government announced that it would definitively evacuate the Rhineland by the end of June; and third, Briand once more signalled that France was interested in improving relations with Germany by circulating his plan for closer union in Europe. He had sketched his idea for the first time at the tenth session of the Assembly of the League of Nations in September of 1929: 'I think that among peoples constituting geographical groups, like the peoples of Europe, there should be some kind of federal bond; it should be possible for them to get in touch at any time, to confer about their interests, to agree on joint resolutions and to establish among themselves a bond of solidarity which will enable them, if need be, to meet any grave emergency that may arise. That is the link I want to forge. Obviously, this association will be primarily economic, for that is the most urgent aspect of the question, and I think we may look for success in that direction.' His speech sparked enormous enthusiasm among the delegates. Now he wanted to take the first concrete steps towards a rapprochement.[33]

Even in the United States, where the economic crisis had been severe, the mood was improving. The decline in industrial production had come to a halt, and since December 1929, the Dow Jones Industrial Average had been climbing (Fig. 3.1). In early March 1930, US President Hoover told the press: 'All the facts indicate that the worst effects of the crash on employment will have been

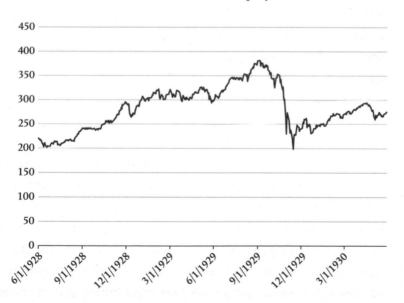

Fig. 3.1 Dow Jones Industrial Average Index, June 1928 to May 1930

passed during the next 30 to 60 days. The resumption of employment throughout the seasonal trades, with the spring, the gradual strengthening of the various forces of recovery, and the successful and active work of the agencies that have been cooperating in restoration are all finding fine results, and I believe will remedy a very large portion of the existing hardship and distress.'[34]

Of course, not everybody shared Hoover's optimism, and the number of people sceptical of the new President had grown considerably since he took office in March 1929. In his public appearances, Hoover failed to connect with the people who were suffering from economic hardship, but at this early stage of the slump, there was a sense that the President knew what he was talking about. The tall, assertive, and hard-working Republican could still build on his reputation as an experienced engineer, an efficient administrator, and a devout Quaker who undertook humanitarian work. Born in 1874 and an orphan from the age of 10, he had left the United States as a 23-year-old to work for the British gold mining company Bewick, Moreing & Co. in Australia and China. Back in the USA in 1900, he worked as a leading mining consultant, investing in all continents and regularly travelling around the globe, and became very wealthy. After the outbreak of war in 1914, Hoover organized large-scale relief efforts, first to the Belgian population, then to millions of war victims. In 1917, he became head of the newly founded US Food and Drug Administration. After the war, he led the American Relief Administration that organized the transport of food to Central Europe. In 1921, he became Secretary of Commerce, a post he held for eight years. He also successfully managed the relief effort following the Great Mississippi Flood of 1927. In 1928, when he ran for President, the Republicans promoted his candidacy with the campaign film 'Herbert Hoover: Master of

Emergencies'. To Hoover, the economic crisis was yet another emergency to be mastered, and the first signs of a recovery reinforced his feeling that he was the right man to navigate the nation through difficult times. After the crash of October 1929, he had encouraged public authorities, railway companies, and utilities to increase their construction programmes and private business leaders to maintain wages. These measures appeared to be successful in cushioning the crisis. Such was the reputation of the President that even the *New York Times*, a supporter of Hoover's opponent Al Smith in the presidential elections of 1928, acknowledged that '[s]ome of the signs of improvement to which the President points are undeniable. He has gathered from official sources many facts going to show that the strain of unemployment is less, and that many lines of business are planning renewed activity. It is right for him to point out these encouragements. He does not do it to promote a foolish optimism but to stimulate confidence in the future and to strengthen the resolution to press forward hopefully.'[35]

Only in Great Britain was there little reason for optimism. The economy had never fully recovered from the war and was mired in recession. Moreover, the minority government formed by the Labour Party under Ramsay MacDonald with the Liberals was beginning to be challenged by internal divisions. In May, Oswald Mosley, a rising star within the Labour Party, who advocated import tariffs, nationalization of industries, and a public works programme to reduce unemployment, left his ministerial position in protest against the austerity policy of the cabinet. He would later become the leading figure of the British fascist movement. Yet, even in Great Britain the political situation was still under control. There was no social unrest on a large scale or any sign of rapid radicalization of the electorate.

Thus, in spring 1930, the economic situation was sobering, but a feeling of guarded optimism started to gain traction among the elites. If Brüning managed to restructure Germany's public finances, the French economy continued to be robust, and the American recovery gained pace, the world economy would leave the crisis behind in the course of the year, carrying the British economy along.

PART II

INDECISION

4

HITLER'S VICTORY

Predictions that the economic crisis was coming to an end turned out to be completely wrong. International trade, industrial production, employment—every major economic indicator resumed its decline. The Fed and other central banks were forced to ease monetary conditions even further. By the end of June 1930, nominal interest rates were at their lowest levels since the end of the war. Share prices on the New York Stock Exchange, after rising from mid-November 1929 to mid-April 1930, resumed their downward trend. Looking back at the economic figures covering the first five months of the year, the *New York Times* wrote: 'If these "factual reports" are left to speak for themselves, they appear to tell rather a gloomy story. In almost every branch of constructive work, manufacture, mining and transportation, percentages of decline are noted, and the seasonal gains which were counted upon have not been realized.'[1]

Soon, other bad news followed. In mid-June, US President Hoover, ignoring the warnings of more than a thousand American economists, signed the protectionist Smoot–Hawley Tariff Act into law sponsored by two Republicans, Senator Reed Smoot and Representative Willis C. Hawley. Its principal element was to increase import duties by an average of 20 per cent. While this would be less harmful than many observers assumed at the time, it sent a negative signal across the world. *The Economist*, a liberal stronghold, was in disbelief: '[W]e have the spectacle of a great country, at a moment of severe trade depression, and faced with a growing necessity to export her manufactures, deliberately erecting barriers against trade with the rest of the world.'[2]

Meanwhile on the eastern side of the Atlantic, Franco-German relations deteriorated as the day of the agreed removal of French troops from the Rhineland approached. French generals brought up one unexpected technical problem after another. Brüning became increasingly impatient, complaining that the mood was 'strained to the extreme by the excessive pedantry of French military officers'. Eventually, the British intervened in support of the Germans. The Labour government, unlike its Conservative predecessor that had been voted out of office in May 1929, endorsed a rapid rehabilitation of Germany at the expense of Britain's special relationship with France. In late April 1930, Foreign Secretary Henderson urged the British ambassador in Paris to put pressure on the French authorities. A delay, he feared, 'may have wider repercussions and make more difficult the smooth and loyal execution of the Young Plan'.[3]

Eventually, the French army left the Rhineland on schedule. When the evacuation took place on 30 June, it was France's turn to feel duped. Instead of praising the event as a further step towards reconciliation, President Hindenburg and the Brüning cabinet only paid tribute to the Germans who had given their lives for the liberty of the fatherland and expressed their hope that France would soon give back the Saar. The proclamation ended with a rallying cry to national strength: 'Let our resolve in this solemn hour be a resolve for unity. Let us unite in an effort after years of tribulation to restore better and brighter days to our beloved fatherland by peaceful means. Let us all unite in the cry: "Deutschland, Deutschland über alles!" [4]

In a similar vein, the Reichswehr held a mass meeting in a stadium in Berlin, attended by thousands of people responding enthusiastically to nationalist slogans. In a rally in the centre of Berlin, even the Reichsbanner, an organization founded by the republican parties, celebrated the de-annexation of the Rhineland and sang the national anthem. On the next day, the Reichswehr fired a twenty-one-gun salute in the Lustgarten next to the City Palace where Prussian kings and German emperors had resided. It was the first military salute since the Kaiser's birthday in January 1914. [5]

The Brüning cabinet decided to circulate a coin bearing the provocative legend: 'The Rhine, Germany's river, not Germany's border.' Foreign Minister Curtius had opposed the decision, but to no avail. Then it was announced that President Hindenburg would travel through the 'liberated' areas in mid-July. He would stay in the Grand Ducal Palace in Mainz, once used by Napoleon Bonaparte, and where the French military headquarters had been located. [6]

Le Temps, the French pro-government newspaper, was deeply disappointed: 'The proclamation of President Hindenburg and the ministers of the Reich does not contain one word about the improved prospects for a rapprochement with France that was supposed to be a logical result of the evacuation of the Rhineland.' The British were taken aback as well. Ambassador Rumbold cabled from Berlin to London: 'The manifesto appears to me to exemplify two of the besetting weaknesses of the German character; ingratitude and tactlessness.' He was particularly concerned about the reference to the Saar: 'It is an unattractive feature of the

German character to display little gratitude for favours received, but when the receipt of favours is followed up by fresh demands, there are grounds for feeling impatient.'[7]

Things got worse. The evacuation was followed by acts of revenge against Germans who had advocated a separation of the Rhineland. The Associated Press reported that in Kaiserslauten three people were seriously injured and a home was burned. 'For more than an hour the police were wholly unable to cope with disorderly elements.' Similar events took place in Mainz. Under the headline 'Indiscriminate lynch law', the *Vossische Zeitung* described rioting against people who were suspected of being separatists. 'Although threats, placards on houses, and the sudden appearance of miniature coffins indicated trouble was coming, the police did nothing to prevent the riots.' Similar events were reported in Wiesbaden.[8]

After these violent clashes, French public opinion turned from disappointment to disgust. Abandoning its measured tone, *Le Temps* wrote of 'odious excesses'. The shock on the French side was understandable. Withdrawing the troops from the Rhineland posed an enormous security risk. France had given up her buffer zone that had served as a sort of insurance mechanism against a potential German attack. The hope was that this act of evacuation would strengthen mutual trust, but the German reaction completely changed the rules of engagement. From the French perspective, Berlin had mistaken her compromise for weakness.[9]

The French reaction was particularly intense, as the issue of an early withdrawal from the Rhineland had always been controversial in domestic politics. When, at the First Hague Conference in August 1929, French Foreign Minister Briand, who was then also Prime Minister, ceded to British and German pressure to withdraw, he promptly lost his majority in the Senate and had to step down as Prime Minister. Using this political momentum, his successor, André Tardieu, immediately accelerated the construction of fortifications stretching from the border with Switzerland in the south to Luxemburg in the north. The project had been developed over the course of the 1920s and was known as the Maginot Line, after the French Minister of War, André Maginot. Both the Chamber of Deputies and the Senate passed the law accelerating its construction in late December 1929, with over 90 per cent of the votes.

Like the British, Tardieu and Maginot were also aware of Germany's secret rearmament plans. In February 1930, General Milne, Chief of the Imperial General Staff, wrote a memorandum ending with warning words: 'Outwardly they are observing to a large extent the dictates of the Treaty of Versailles, but at the same time they are endeavouring by secret means to evade the restrictions imposed by that Treaty, with a view to laying the foundations for a large expansion at some future date when the political situation may permit it. Their immediate objectives, therefore, are not to prepare the present German Army for war, but to organize the nation as a whole, and industry in particular, so that it may be ready once more to convert itself into a war machine should the necessity arise, and in the meantime to prevent the military spirit from dying out in Germany.'[10]

In this heated atmosphere, it was clear that Paris had to take diplomatic action. The cabinet instructed French ambassador Pierre de Margerie in Berlin to deliver a démarche to the German government. Leopold von Hoesch, the German ambassador in Paris, briefly cooled this escalation by having his government point out in an official response that France had financed separatist movements in the occupied Rhineland in 1923. Still, when delivering his message to Foreign Minister Curtius, the French ambassador obviously did not hold back. Curtius put on record after the meeting that 'the dispute threatened to reach the limit of what was tolerable'. Franco-German relations had reached a new nadir.[11]

The French were irritated by other events in Germany. Before travelling to the 'liberated' cities in the west, President Hindenburg urged the Prussian government to suspend the ban that had been imposed on the 'Steel Helmet' in the Rhineland and Westphalia in October 1929 in reaction to illegal military exercises. 'Steel Helmet' was a revanchist paramilitary organization of former front-line soldiers founded in November 1918. It had moved to the far Right since 1929 and Hindenburg was an honorary member. The Prussian government headed by the Social Democrat Otto Braun eventually gave in after Hindenburg threatened to cancel his trip to the Rhineland. On 16 July, the ban was officially suspended.[12]

The French were also disillusioned by the German response to Briand's 'Memorandum on the Organization of a System of Federal European Union'. It was not so much that the German government expressed reservations. Other governments, especially the British and the Italian one, were sceptical as well. But the tone of the German note and the idea of linking the support of Briand's plan to a revision of the Versailles Treaty offended the French government. Obviously, German foreign policy had entered a new phase. Up until the surrender of the Rhineland, Berlin still had an interest in talking to Paris. Once this goal had been attained, the German government felt free to ignore French interests and to pursue a more aggressive foreign policy. To support the new course,

Brüning made an important change in the Ministry for Foreign Affairs. State Secretary Carl von Schubert, a strong supporter of Franco-German cooperation, was replaced by Bernhard von Bülow, a nephew of the former Chancellor Bülow, who had always opposed the policy of rapprochement. On 2 June, he took office at the Wilhelmstrasse.[13]

Amidst this growing political mistrust, the flotation of the Young Bond produced disappointing results. Its price in the market quickly slid below the offer price of 90 per cent of face value. The view that the Young Plan would give a boost to the world economy turned out to be a pipe dream. *Der Deutsche Volkswirt*, Germany's leading economic magazine, was alarmed: 'The failure of the Young Bond flotation is not an insignificant event that concerns only a few investors. German credit is damaged by it in a form that is irreparable for the time being.'[14]

The main reason for the bad reception of the Young Bond was Germany's deteriorating fiscal situation. By early May, it had become evident that the number of unemployed was much higher and tax receipts much lower than expected. As a result, the Unemployment Insurance Fund continued to be deep in the red. Municipalities were in financial trouble as well. It was estimated that another RM 750 million, i.e. nearly 10 per cent of the annual budget of the Reich, would be needed to restore public finances. Finance Minister Paul Moldenhauer was forced to prepare an austerity budget. On 10 May, his State Secretary, Hans Schäffer, had a long private conversation with Chancellor Brüning and pressured him to take action before July. Brüning ceded.[15]

In the following weeks, the cabinet held one meeting after another to hammer out ways to scrape together the money. On 6 June, the press was informed of a new three-part plan. First, to strengthen the Unemployment Insurance Fund, it proposed an increase of workers' contributions from 3.5 to 4.5 per cent of salaries and some savings reforms. Second, to boost revenues, it recommended a temporary 4 per cent emergency tax for employees with a fixed salary in both the public and private sectors as well as a 10 per cent tax increase for unmarried persons and a higher tax on bonuses paid to members of boards of directors. In addition, the government would try to sell preference shares of the Reichsbahn and increase the income from cigarette taxes by changing the payment schedule. Third, the plan proposed a series of spending cuts, notably of health insurance compensations and of revenues apportioned to states and municipalities. To mitigate the contractionary effect of all these measures, the cabinet promised to invest hundreds of millions of Reichsmarks in job creation schemes.[16]

Predictably, this austerity plan was very unpopular. *Vorwärts*, the party organ of the Social Democrats, asked indignantly: 'Where is the majority for all this?' Even the centre-right German People's Party (DVP), the party of Finance Minister Paul Moldenhauer who was the architect of the austerity programme, did not support it. The DVP deputies were particularly upset about the 4 per cent emergency tax because it affected their voter base disproportionately. In mid-June, after the cabinet officially backed the Moldenhauer plan, the DVP deputies decided to push him out of office. Moldenhauer folded, offering his resignation at a cabinet meeting on 18 June. 'I don't have the public behind me', he explained. 'I have lost any credibility.'[17]

The early resignation of the Finance Minister boded ill for the chances of the technocratic Brüning cabinet to push its austerity package through the Reichstag. The end of the Grand Coalition in March 1930 had been preceded by the resignation of Finance Minister Hilferding in December 1929. Would history repeat itself?

Moldenhauer's successor was Hermann Dietrich, the Vice-Chancellor of the Brüning cabinet. Dietrich was more cheerful and energetic than Moldenhauer. Born in 1879 in the Grand Duchy of Baden, the south-west corner of the German Empire, he studied law and became a career politician before he turned 30, first as mayor of a town in the region, then, during the war, as Senior Mayor of Konstanz. After the war, he joined the government of Baden for two years and then became member of the Reichstag for the left-liberal Deutsche Demokratische Partei (DDP). In 1928, he was named Minister of Food and Agriculture in the Grand Coalition. When Brüning became Chancellor in March 1930, he was posted to the Ministry of Economic Affairs. And now, in June 1930, he took over the helm at the Finance Ministry and faced the toughest job of his career.[18]

Despite his talents, Dietrich was a controversial candidate for the Finance Ministry. He lacked consistency, both in terms of policy and leadership. He was notorious for his angry outbursts. German senior officials called him 'the rumbling god' and 'the peasant from Waldgutach' (his home town). Dietrich knew everything about the German forest and allegedly could catch trout by hand, but he was incapable of understanding the dynamics of the economic crisis. On top of that, his anti-Semitism precipitated repeated clashes with his Jewish State Secretary, Hans Schäffer, who was much more knowledgeable on fiscal policy issues. Dietrich and Schäffer shared the conviction that the Nazis should be kept out of the bureaucracy, but they were not a strong team.[19]

Although he threw himself into the fray with great enthusiasm and readjusted the austerity programme, Dietrich soon ran aground just as his predecessor Moldenhauer had. As his negotiations with party leaders were to reveal, there was no majority in the Reichstag in favour of another round of austerity. Yet Brüning was not willing to restart the whole process: 'If the cabinet falters now, then we will have an economic catastrophe', he warned his ministers. 'I don't expect anything from further negotiations with the parties. I am not willing to put myself in an impossible situation and be ambushed. I will head off the fight in the Reichstag.'[20]

Brüning's principled approach had no effect on the opposition. On 16 July, at noon, the Reichstag delivered its verdict: 256 out of 449 deputies rejected the emergency levy on salaried workers, thus effectively burying the whole austerity plan. The opposition consisted of an 'unholy alliance' of Social Democrats, Communists, and the extreme Right, i.e. Hugenberg's DNVP and the Nazis. The Left criticized the cuts in social services and called for higher taxes on the upper income brackets, while the Right wanted to precipitate the fall of the government and create economic chaos. Yet, Brüning still would not budge. He knew he had the authority from President Hindenburg to enforce his austerity plan by invoking Article 48 of the Weimar Constitution and to dissolve the Reichstag if it rejected the recourse to this article. And so it was that a few hours after the defeat, the cabinet made the austerity measures effective by invoking Article 48.[21]

The Social Democrats immediately introduced a bill calling for the application of Article 48 to be rejected. They believed that compromising on austerity would undermine their credibility as the main representatives of the Left. 'It is about the matter of the working class', the party organ *Vorwärts* wrote. 'Brüning's policy is class struggle from above.' They also knew that if they endorsed Brüning they would lose at the ballot box to the Communists.

On 18 July, the Reichstag reconvened to debate and vote on the Social Democrats' bill. Up until the last moment, it was not clear whether Brüning or the Social Democrats would prevail. Then, shortly before 1 p.m., the President of the Reichstag announced that 236 deputies had voted in favour of the rejection of Article 48, with 221 opposed. Again, the 'unholy alliance' prevailed, although some members of Hugenberg's DNVP had deserted. 'Bravo!', the Nazis shouted, as Chancellor Brüning stepped up to the podium to read President Hindenburg's decree proclaiming the dissolution of the Reichstag. Now the Communists were shouting, 'Down with this hunger government!' After Brüning ended his short statement, the President of the Reichstag concluded the session with the succinct sentence: 'Therewith, our work here is ended.'[22]

A few minutes later, the cabinet convened in a room of the parliament building and scheduled elections for 14 September. They also decided to ask President Hindenburg to issue new emergency decrees enacting the austerity package. Such a manoeuvre was legal, as long as the Reichstag was dissolved. As promised, Hindenburg endorsed Brüning. On 26 July, he decreed the budget for the year 1930, new taxes, and an increase of contributions to the Unemployment Insurance Fund. A fiscal crisis was thus avoided, but at the price of a full-blown political crisis.[23]

As with the end of the Grand Coalition in March 1930, contemporaries strongly disagreed as to whether the dissolution of the Reichstag in July 1930 had been inevitable. Some blamed Brüning for not trying hard enough to strike a deal with the Social Democrats. Others singled out the Social Democrats for their refusal to defend the parliamentary system, just as they had refused to support the Grand Coalition in March 1930. The *Vossische Zeitung*, the mouthpiece of the Brüning cabinet, wrote in its editorial: 'The Social Democrats have provided evidence that you cannot govern without them. But at what price! They extorted the dissolution of the Reichstag with the help of the mortal enemies of democracy: the Communists, the National Socialists, and the entourage of Hugenberg.'[24]

But there is reason to believe, as some historians now do, that Brüning had little choice. The gap formed by the DVP pulling to the right and the Social Democrats pulling to the left had become too large. On 15 July, one day before the austerity package was rejected in the Reichstag, the Chancellor had asked his ministers what to do if the Social Democrats indicated they were ready to negotiate. Only one minister thought that it would be a good idea to move towards their position. All others believed that this tactical change would be fruitless. Brüning shared this view, arguing that '[t]he centre-right parties would stop supporting us'.[25]

In any case, the technocrat who was supposed to clean up the fiscal mess had failed. And as if the situation had not been bad enough, shocking news came in from Koblenz where President Hindenburg was making a stop on his trip through the 'liberated' Rhineland. On 22 July, late in the evening, after marvelling at the fireworks launched from the elevated Ehrenbreitstein fortress, some 200 people fell into the river after a floating bridge collapsed, with 35 of them drowning. Hindenburg stopped his trip abruptly and returned to Berlin.[26]

In contrast to the fall of the Grand Coalition, the dissolution of the Reichstag had a severely negative impact on financial markets. Investors began to realize that Germany was politically unstable. Already in the week before Brüning went down fighting in the

Reichstag, the German central bank lost nearly RM 240 million, 8 per cent of its total gold and foreign exchange reserves. And in the week after the dissolution of the Reichstag the Young Bond listed in Amsterdam fell by more than four percentage points. The decline then slowed, stabilizing in mid-August until the elections in mid-September.[27]

The foreign press was also more alarmed than when the Grand Coalition fell. *The Economist* spoke of a 'formidable political crisis in Germany, which seems likely to have far-reaching effects'. It also warned of the political risks of the economic crisis: 'The election campaign will not be very pleasant, in view of the severe economic distress which is causing great unrest everywhere.' *The Times* pointed to the international dimension of what had happened in Berlin: 'The financial and economic stability of Germany is of course a matter of concern not to Germany alone; for this and for other reasons the nature of the emergency measures and the outcome of the appeal to the electorate will be watched with unusual attention abroad.' In Paris, *Le Temps* was concerned about the degradation of German democracy: 'Every party is focussed mainly on defending the interests of its electoral clientele.'[28]

French diplomats and ministers were also increasingly alarmed. On 25 July, the French financial attaché in Berlin cabled to Paris: 'I would not like to be too pessimistic . . . I would not like to upset Paris too much . . . [but] I cannot prevent myself from seeing the situation in black colours . . .' Even the French ambassador in Berlin, Pierre de Margerie, not an expert in economic affairs, began to understand that Germany had entered dangerous territory. Alarmed by de Margerie's dispatches from Berlin, Foreign Minister Briand wrote to Finance Minister Reynaud after the dissolution of the Reichstag: 'At this point, one finds oneself facing nothing.'[29]

Thus, by the summer of 1930, the mood had changed dramatically. The year began with the Young Plan being hailed euphorically as a new step towards European peace. Now, disappointment, mistrust, and fear prevailed.[30]

How would Brüning do at the elections? In early August, while vacationing in a chalet in the Swiss resort of Saas-Fee, State Secretary Hans Schäffer set out his predictions in a long letter to the Hamburg banker Max Warburg. Schäffer expected that the National Socialists would gain forty seats, Hugenberg's DNVP thirty seats, and the Communists fifty-five seats. Sir Horace Rumbold, the British ambassador in Berlin, wrote to Foreign Secretary Henderson in early September that the National Socialists 'are confident that in the election they will gain over 3 million votes and some fifty or sixty seats in the Reichstag. To me, personally, this number seems somewhat high, and it may be assumed that the National Socialists' own estimates would be on the high side.' And after having cast his ballot, the Chief of Staff of the Chancellery, Hermann Pünder, predicted that the Communists would win fifty seats, the extreme Right consisting of the NSDAP and the DNVP one hundred seats.[31]

When the results came in late in the night, it was clear that even the pessimists had been too optimistic. The Communists won 75 seats, the NSDAP and the DNVP together 148 seats, with the Nazis winning 107 and the DNVP 41 seats. The NSDAP was now the second largest party in the Reichstag behind the Social Democrats (143 seats). In 1928, it had been an obscure fringe party, winning only 2.6 per cent (Table 4.1). Pünder was devastated: 'An absolutely horrible result!' 'A victory of radicalism', the *Vossische Zeitung* wrote.[32]

Table 4.1 Results of Reichstag elections, 1928–1932

	20 May 1928		14 Sept. 1930		31 July 1932		6 Nov. 1932	
	In %	Seats	In %	Seats	In %	Seats	In %	Seats
Communists (KPD)	10.6	54	13.1	77	14.6	89	16.9	100
Social Democrats (SPD)	29.8	153	24.5	143	21.6	133	20.4	121
Centre Party (Zentrum)	12.1	62	11.8	68	12.5	75	11.9	70
Bavarian Party (BVP)	3.1	16	3.0	10	3.2	22	3.1	20
Democrats (DDP)	4.9	24	3.8	20	1.0	4	1.0	2
People's Party (DVP)	8.7	45	4.5	30	1.2	7	1.9	11
National People's Party (DNVP)	14.2	73	7.0	41	5.9	37	8.8	52
Nazi Party (NSDAP)	2.6	12	18.3	107	37.4	230	33.1	196
Rest	13.9	31	14.0	72	2.6	11	2.9	12
Total		491		577		608		584

Source. Statistisches Reichsamt.

Of the ruling coalition, only Brüning's Centre Party could avoid losing seats, but it had now even fewer than the Communists. Furthermore, the turnout was very high (82 per cent), meaning that there was no silent majority supporting Brüning's course. On the contrary, many new voters went to the polls to express their anger with the state of affairs. Parliamentary support for the government had shrunk dramatically. Brüning could govern only if the Social Democrats supported him, but President Hindenburg was strongly against them joining the government.[33]

There were many reasons for the Nazi victory, above all the economic crisis and the ensuing political discontent. Also, they had run a well-organized campaign with modern propaganda tools. Hitler's charisma ensured an appeal to all classes with its promise to restore Germany's greatness and power. But the single most important factor was that the Nazis succeeded in blaming the Young Plan for the domestic economic crisis. By focusing on this issue the Nazis projected a view that was shared by a large majority of the German population. Even the Socialist labour unions were in favour of a revision of the Young Plan. Moreover, the link between the Young Plan and the domestic economic crisis was not wrong. Germany found itself in a debt trap that partially resulted from the reparations regime. It became easy to blame the creditor countries.

In his very first campaign speech, given only a few hours after the dissolution of the Reichstag at a Nazi rally in Munich, Hitler singled out the Young Plan as the symbol of failure of the Weimar elites:

> Of course, the Young Plan is not the only crime, but it is the most recent one and the most clearly visible one, and the pitcher goes often to the well and gets broken at last—and it should get broken! We will make sure in the campaign that the failures of Germany's spoilers will be clearly teased out so that they cannot absolve themselves from them through gimmickry or absent themselves.[34]

Ten days later, at a rally of Nazi Party leaders, Hitler sketched out his campaign plan: 'By adopting the Young Plan, Marxism and the bourgeoisie are guilty in the same way. This enables the N.S.D.A.P. to mount the severest and most ruthless offensive against the arrayed forces of the Young parties.'[35] Joseph Goebbels, the Nazi campaign manager, seized the point immediately and guided the party speakers to focus on reparations. By contrast, diatribes against the Jews at that time were relatively rare. To be sure, anti-Semitism was ever-present in the Nazi campaign, or was mixed with the attack on the 'Young parties' (Illustration 9). People who voted for Hitler knew that he blamed the Jews for the misery of the nation and they approved it. But it was not the main issue that mobilized voters in such a high number.[36]

Hitler's focus on the Young Plan wrong-footed Brüning. The Chancellor had hoped the elections would be a referendum on his economic policies, and he firmly believed that a majority of voters would recognize that he was the best man to clean up the financial mess. But that debate did not happen. On 20 August, Brüning warned his ministers that 'foreign policy has been largely hijacked by the National Socialists'. He therefore appealed to them 'to be as prudent as possible in their statements about foreign policy issues'. Brüning was cornered in a political arena where he could not fight with full force. If he supported the abolishment of reparations, he would unsettle foreign investors; if he fought against the popular campaign for an end of reparations, he was sure to lose the elections.[37]

In its editorial after the elections, *Le Temps* nicely summarized the dynamics of the German elections: 'The German people were called to pass judgment on the financial and fiscal policies of the Brüning cabinet. But, from the first day of the electoral campaign, this issue was somehow relegated to the second rank. Nobody had any interest in touching such a delicate issue, as it was about asking the popular masses for new sacrifices and imposing new burdens on them... Under these conditions it is hardly surprising that we saw an electoral campaign that was about the foreign

Illustration 9. Election poster of NSDAP in September 1930: 'Punch them out' (top left), 'the Young parties' (bottom left), 'Elect list 9—National Socialists'.

policy of the Reich, a subject that allowed all groups to outbid themselves in giving vent to the most outrageous demagoguery, knowing that this way they could appeal to the emotions of the whole of the electoral clientele.'[38]

The Nazis were particularly strong in Protestant northern and eastern Germany, especially in the countryside. In some rural areas, they achieved more than 50 per cent of the vote. But their real success consisted in mobilizing people from all walks of life, with many of them first-time voters. Even the female electorate, traditionally reluctant to vote for radical parties, now voted for the Nazis to the same extent as men. Hitler's party was underrepresented in the working classes, industrial cities, and Catholic regions. However, the more remarkable result of the September elections was that the Nazis gained a foothold even in the milieu that had been the turf of the Communists, the Social Democrats, and the Catholic Centre Party. They had managed to form a movement that attracted all groups protesting the failure of the Weimar Republic.[39]

A journalist of the *Vossische Zeitung* who visited the celebrations of the NSDAP in Berlin was surprised by the broad range of Nazi supporters who celebrated with Joseph Goebbels 'The National Socialists of Berlin had secured the big hall of the Sportpalast, in order to celebrate their electoral success on Sunday night. The celebration proceeded loudly, with great rejoicing. The party supporters had come in families, some with their children, and were seated on the tables on the floor that were erected instead of the usual rows of chairs.'

The journalist continues with a long, almost stream-of-consciousness description of the event and its atmosphere:

Enthusiastic response when Dr Goebbels, leader of the Berlin National Socialists, appears. He speaks, but does not make any precise statements about the future policy of his party. Between the speeches always music. Festive mood, fraternization. People wave the little red flags with the swastika and are in good spirits.

Many employees are there, presumably also civil servants and particularly many women, young women, students, salespersons. Maybe they were fired, maybe their salary had been cut, now they all expect salvation, economic salvation from Hitler. There is also a strikingly large number of well-dressed older couples who quite evidently belong to the upper middle class, the men sometimes decorated with medals. Defecting friends of Hugenberg who follow the more strident key.

So, all of them, differently situated socially and economically, cheered Goebbels who has been busy for the last one and a half hours writing his name on hundreds of picture postcards. Entranced young girls look at him. He is the star of the electoral campaign in Berlin. And, smiling, he allows himself to receive rose bouquets, to be carried out of the hall on the arms of his young men and to be put in the marvelous black Mercedes car whose radiator almost disappears under the arbour.

Then they disperse. The security police teams that kept the Sportpalast under guard within a wide radius did not have a hard job.[40]

The next day, the party propaganda chief wrote in his diary about the same event: 'Our people go completely wild. Excitement like 1914. The Sportpalast resembles a madhouse.'[41]

5

TO THE BRINK AND BACK

Chancellor Brüning was highly embarrassed by the election results. Back in July he had assumed that the elections would widen his political support. Instead, the opposite happened, and his government was weaker than ever. On Monday morning after election day, he informally met with a few ministers to discuss the new situation. The mood was both depressed and defiant, as one participant observed: 'The men all had long faces, and there was obviously the feeling that something had to be done, no matter what.'[1]

Eventually they decided to use a more aggressive language on the diplomatic scene, since everybody agreed that the Young Plan had been the root cause of the electoral defeat. Brüning sent Prelate Kaas, the chairman of his party, to Geneva to urge Foreign Minister Curtius to speak out aggressively at the meeting of the Council of the League of Nations. The initiative completely backfired. The Foreign Minister, offended by the intrusion of the Prelate, refused to revise his speech. He felt that 'people in Berlin lost their heads' and considered the idea to change tack feckless. 'And then what?', he asked Mr Kaas, who was stuck for an answer. Curtius explained that he would leave Geneva 'if the Chancellor insisted on these ideas'. Kaas retreated and took the plane back to Berlin the next morning, while Curtius gave the speech he had always intended to give.[2]

The only good news of the day was that Brüning received the backing of President Hindenburg whom he met after sending Kaas to the airport. 'Continue to work calmly and soberly', the old Field Marshall told the former front-line officer. But the presidential support did not unmake the victory of the Nazis and the Communists. The ruling parties assembled fewer than 200 votes in the Reichstag; they needed 288 for a majority. There seemed to be no way forward.[3]

The next morning, Brüning gathered his cabinet for the first formal meeting since the elections. The Chancellor, still in pessimistic mood, had little to offer. His only message was that he would not resign. 'Some people take the view that we should cede the responsibility to Hugenberg and the National Socialists, because under such circumstances the nimbus around these parties would soon disappear. For constitutional reasons, I cannot share this view.' Consequently, the only option was an informal coalition with the Social Democrats. They had let him down in July when he wanted to pass the austerity programme. Would they follow him this time? There was little reason to be optimistic. The Social Democrats had lost votes to the Communists in the September elections, making it harder for them to cosy up to the austere Chancellor.[4]

After Brüning, Finance Minister Dietrich described the fiscal situation, making clear that the outlook was now even gloomier. He revealed that in August the funding gap had become much wider than anticipated. Thus, once more, the government would run out of cash if it did not implement another austerity programme. 'We can maintain our payment schedule until mid-December', he told his colleagues. 'What will happen then, I cannot foresee.' Labour Minister Stegerwald confirmed Dietrich's view. The Unemployment Insurance Fund was deteriorating much faster than expected and would soon be 'highly critical' again, he told the cabinet. Another increase in workers' contributions was needed, and that would make collaboration with the Social Democrats even more unlikely.[5]

Investors too were shattered. The *Vossische Zeitung* described the scene at the stock exchange the morning after the elections. 'Bank managers, bankers and traders went to the Burgstrasse earlier than usual, and it was striking to see that the so-called "first class" was already in the spotlight, even before official trading began. One could see everywhere agitated groups deep in discussions. Of course, the market had expected an extreme election result, but the outcome has thrown all calculations into disarray.' When the trading floor opened, some shares at the Berlin stock exchange lost up to 20 per cent. It felt like a liquidation sale.[6]

Yet, surprisingly, the sell-out was only temporary. As early as Monday afternoon, share prices recovered and continued to rise for another two days. On Wednesday evening, they were nearly at the same level as a week earlier. Obviously, a sort of consensus view emerged that the Weimar Republic was still resilient enough to withstand the advance of the radical opposition parties. Even foreign investors, especially from the United States and Switzerland, returned to the market and bought German securities.[7]

The recovery was not to last, however. Markets were in a manic-depressive mood. On Friday, investors were seized by a new wave of pessimism after German newspapers spread a rumour of an impending Nazi putsch in Prussia. Brüning tried to calm the markets by telling American journalists that the rumour was false. And the Prussian government publicly denied the press reports. It was to no avail. The City and Wall Street witnessed a dramatic sell-out of German securities. According to the *New York Times*, this led to the 'sharpest decline since early August'. In addition, the Reichsbank suffered from a drain of foreign reserves (Fig. 5.1). Brüning, who was already preoccupied with political gridlock and a widening funding gap, now had to cope with a looming currency crisis. Germany's plight became ever more critical by the day.[8]

On Monday morning, 22 September 1930, Brüning held a meeting with Finance Minister Dietrich, State Secretary Schäffer, and President of the Reichsbank Luther. Schäffer explained that they desperately needed a foreign loan to prevent a collapse. He believed $100 million to $125 million was needed and considered two years as the maximum maturity they could demand in the current crisis environment. They all agreed. Schäffer also suggested setting up a debt redemption scheme, thus making sure that the loan would be repaid on schedule. Again, there was a broad consensus. Finally, they decided to hammer out a new austerity programme as soon as possible. To close the funding gap, they needed to reduce the

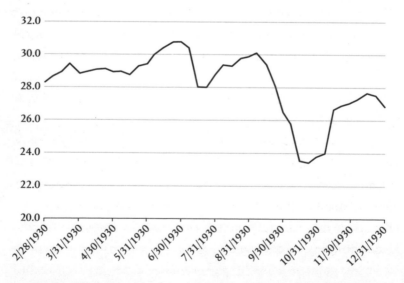

Fig. 5.1 Total reserves of Reichsbank (in billions of Reichsmark)

deficit during the current fiscal year to 31 March 1931, and seek a balanced budget during the following year.[9]

It was a Herculean task. Would Brüning succeed? Hermann Pünder, the State Secretary of the Chancellery, was pessimistic. He believed that Germany was going through its worst period since 1918, even taking the hyperinflation years into account: 'I see the future with greater anxiety than ever before. The situation today is not comparable with any time since the war. Even in the inflation period 1923/24 it was better insofar as the people who suffered from great losses of their fortune understood that something drastic had to be done whereas this is not the case today.'[10]

The priority was to find a bank willing to lend to Germany. Again, Schäffer took the initiative. He remembered a conversation with George Murnane of the Boston-based investment bank, Lee, Higginson & Co., in the summer before the elections. At the time, Schäffer (Illustration 10) declined to consider the financial help offered, but left a door open in case Germany's finances deteriorated further. This moment had arrived, since there was no realistic alternative. The City of London signalled only faint interest, and a deal with Parisian banks was impossible, as long as the French government interfered by imposing political conditions that were not acceptable to Germany.[11]

Yet, given the high degree of political uncertainty in Germany, would Lee, Higginson still be willing to lend to Germany? Murnane at least agreed to enter negotiations. He did this for several reasons. First, the bank had already lent large sums to Germany and was reluctant to risk an early default. Second, the bank, an old, venerable, and leading financial institution in Boston, was still an outsider on Wall Street. Murnane and his partners longed to equal J. P. Morgan, the alpha male of financial diplomacy. Germany, the most

Illustration 10. Hans Schäffer, State Secretary of the German Finance Ministry.

important economy in Europe, appeared to be a particularly lucrative market. Third, in 1929 Lee, Higginson had been instrumental in providing the Swedish 'match king' Ivar Kreuger with the German matchmaking market monopoly in exchange for a $125 million loan to the Reich. The American bankers knew German finance officials quite well and trusted them.[12]

Meanwhile, the flight of capital continued unabated. Brüning was furious, regretting that he did not have the power to control the press: 'The sober analysis of the results that prevailed in the first day after the elections has ceded to a nervous atmosphere lately. It is particularly worrisome that even bond prices have sharply declined. It is distressing that the government has no means of banning the irresponsible press that, for the sake of sensation, fuels anxieties about supposedly imminent putsch attempts.' By Wednesday, 24 September, the Reichsbank's gold and foreign exchange reserves were 10 per cent lower than on election day. Confidence in the German currency had dramatically deteriorated.[13]

Investors were unsettled by further negative news the following day. Coming to the defence of three officers who were accused of high treason for promoting Nazi propaganda within the Reichswehr, Adolf Hitler stated in his testimony at the Supreme Court in Leipzig that 'heads will roll in the sand', once the Nazis were in power. The message sent shock waves across the country. The cabinet even interrupted its meeting to seek confirmation from Leipzig that Hitler had used these words. Share values on the Berlin stock exchange plunged. Later in the day, Wall Street reacted negatively as well.[14]

Negotiations with Lee, Higginson began on Friday, 26 September 1930, nearly two weeks after the elections, with the German side in a very weak position. The American bankers made clear that they wanted high interest rates in return for granting credit to a country in crisis. They also refused to allow repayment after two years and insisted on a scheme with three tranches of six monthly repayments in return for German treasuries as collateral. And to further satisfy themselves that the Reich could service its debt, they sought some commitments from the government on its fiscal policy.[15]

On Sunday, 28 September, Schäffer delivered responses that satisfied the American bankers. Then, entirely unexpectedly, the outlook improved markedly, as French banks showed an interest in participating in the loan. The initiative had been launched by the

Paris subsidiary of Lee, Higginson as part of a strategy of broadening political support for Berlin. It was even backed by the French government which feared that Brüning would seek a moratorium of the Young Plan if the crisis got out of control. Tardieu and Briand also tried to moderate the press and encouraged French banks to stop withdrawing their funds from Germany. There seems to have been a genuine desire to help.[16]

Now negotiations with Lee, Higginson entered the next phase. Once more, the American bankers made clear who was in the driving seat. Besides repeating their claim for a high interest rate of 6 per cent, they demanded that the debt redemption bill be approved by a parliamentary majority, not on the basis of Article 48. The Germans had little choice. On Saturday morning, 4 October, Schäffer pleaded for a quick deal. 'If capital outflows continue at the same speed, German banks will be forced to call in their loans', he warned Brüning and the other ministers. 'That would mean the end for many small and medium-sized enterprises.' The situation had become highly critical. A few days earlier, Ministry of Finance officials had hinted at the possibility that the treasuries due on 6 and 10 October would not be rolled over by Germany's creditors. Finance Minister Dietrich was shattered by that prospect and was about to lose his nerve.[17]

Brüning agreed with Schäffer's proposal to cede to the American bankers' new demands and intended to sign the loan agreement without delay. But, suddenly, the French side asked for additional guarantees that went beyond the parliamentary backing of the debt redemption bill. This was not acceptable to Brüning. To save the deal, the Germans prepared to send a delegation of senior officials to Paris. In a secret memorandum, they made a list of what the German negotiators were supposed to reveal and what they were to hide. The most important point was that there should be no linkage between the austerity package and the foreign loan. 'If the impression emerges', the memo stated, 'that the austerity package was launched as a result of foreign pressure . . . adoption would be impossible. Drastic measures, such as the lowering of civil servants' wages, the curtailing of the autonomy of Länder and municipalities, and the blockage of subsidies to the Unemployment Insurance Fund could never be passed by any parliament in such conditions.' Apparently, Brüning and his confidants had learned from the election experience: never give the opposition the opportunity of blaming the government for caving in to foreigners' demands that would deepen the crisis at home.[18]

Surprisingly, prospects for a deal suddenly improved. The next day, the French government reversed its position and gave the green light to the loan without attaching additional strings to it. It even recommended that two other French banks should participate. The German delegation's trip to Paris was cancelled. Schäffer got the reassuring message that 'only in political circles was there still fear that the money would possibly benefit Hitler'. Financial circles, including the Banque de France, fully backed a deal with Germany, he was told by his source.[19]

In the meantime, the cabinet discussed the austerity measures day and night. On Monday evening, 29 September, it approved a programme. The goal was to reduce the deficit during the current fiscal year and to reach a balanced budget for the fiscal year running from April 1931 to March 1932. It included the lowering of civil servants' salaries by 6 per cent and those of Hindenburg, Brüning, ministers, and parliamentary deputies by 20 per cent. It foresaw a series of spending cuts, an increase of the tobacco tax, and an extension of the controversial 5 per cent emergency levy introduced in the first austerity programme back in July. Altogether, the lowering of wages and the spending cuts created savings of RM 1 billion which corresponded to more than 10 per cent of the budget of the Reich. In addition, workers' contributions to the Unemployment Insurance Fund were immediately raised from 4.5 to 6.5 per cent, and the Reich injected another RM 200 million. To mitigate the contractionary effects of the austerity package, several hundreds of millions of RM were committed to investing in apartment construction and canal building over the course of the next few years.[20]

The next step was to prepare the public for all these cruelties. Brüning encouraged all ministers to soften up journalists in advance of the official announcement. On 1 October, Dietrich and Stegerwald informed the press about the programme. The announcement made a good impression on some American investors, as the German banker Jacob Goldschmidt reported from New York. But domestically, the reaction was harsh. Even the *Vossische Zeitung*, an ally of Brüning, could hardly detect 'to what extent the government was thinking about the parliamentary acceptability of the program'. According to the paper, the cabinet had developed a programme for themselves, although they had only a minority in the Reichstag. 'It is as if a trio played a quartet.' Observing the resistance in political circles, Pünder had reason to stick to his pessimism, writing once more in his diary that he saw the future 'with great anxiety, as never since 1918'.[21]

Brüning met party leaders to find out how he could forge a majority for the austerity package and the debt redemption bill. Increasingly, he got the sense that the Social Democrats might eventually endorse him, although the party was still divided on the austerity measures. Thus, when he met Hitler, Wilhelm Frick, and Gregor Strasser in the apartment of his friend Gottfried Treviranus on Sunday, 6 October 1930, he did not need the cooperation of the Nazis. This put him in a strong position.[22]

Goebbels considered Hitler's meeting with Brüning a big success. He wrote in his diary: 'Waited at home for the call. Late in the evening boss and Frick come back from Brüning. It was a long and principled debate. Treviranus was there as well. We continue our opposition. Thank God. But this Reichstag will have only a short life. Hitler seems to have made a mighty impression on Brüning. He was totally happy. Now things are progressing.'[23]

Brüning drew a completely different picture in his memoirs. He wrote that he had tried to get Hitler interested in his plan to topple the Versailles Treaty by abandoning reparations and tackling the disarmament issue over the course of the next two years. He also explained to him that in the short term Germany needed to obtain a foreign loan in order to prevent a catastrophic financial crisis. Yet, Hitler's response had nothing to do with what Brüning had said. He gave a loud, one-hour speech and became ever louder, as singing SA troops passed by the street of Treviranus's apartment every fifteen minutes. Brüning was not impressed at all:

> He did not enter at all into the fundamental questions of any future policy, namely not into the financial multi-year plan that apparently he did not understand. More and more he used the word 'annihilation', firstly directed against the Social Democrats, then against the reactionary forces and finally against France as the hereditary enemy and Russia as the stronghold of bolshevism.

Brüning's question of how he would obtain the Lee, Higginson loan after the electoral victory of the National Socialists (NSDAP) had already caused a drain of more than half a billion Reichsmark failed to refocus the conversation. Hitler went on with his geopolitical plans and spoke for another hour. Disillusioned, the Chancellor concluded that Hitler would always follow the principle 'first power, then policy' and ended the conversation. Treviranus had the same impression: 'When saying farewell, Hitler promised that his press would not publish any personal attacks against us, the hosts of this meeting. We did not thank him. I did not feel mesmerised at this first meeting; rather, I found the facial traits and the guttural voice as repellent.'[24]

Whether or not Brüning was recording the truth is hard to know, as his memoirs are considered unreliable. But there is no doubt that at the time he saw no common ground with Hitler nor felt any sympathy for his party.[25] Two days later, on 8 October, he explained to President Hindenburg that the Nazis had acted completely irresponsibly by proposing an immediate revision of reparations and declaring a moratorium. 'The National Socialists have a fundamentally different agenda, well knowing that their suggestions would have catastrophic consequences. Cooperation is impossible for the time being.' Brüning was right. Any attempt to raise the reparation issue in the middle of the current crisis would have led to the collapse of the German monetary and financial system. Brüning also dropped a hint to the President that the Social Democrats might endorse him in the Reichstag. Hindenburg signalled that he agreed with the Chancellor's strategy, although he disliked the Left. At last, the political majority that was needed to obtain the foreign loan and to end the crisis seemed near.[26]

Unfortunately, however, on 8 October 1930, the same day Brüning met Hindenburg, the French changed their mind again. Thomas McKittrick from Lee, Higginson in London reported that the French banks could not participate in the loan without the consent of their government. Once more, the French authorities could not resist the temptation to use Germany's dependence on foreign money to impose political conditions. Now, the situation became critical. On Wednesday, 9 October, one day after the French flip-flop, the Reichsbank increased the official interest rate from 4 per cent to 5 per cent to try to stem capital flight. In the three weeks since the elections of mid-September, its gold and foreign exchange reserves had declined from RM 2.94 million to RM 2.35 million corresponding to a loss of around 20 per cent. The cover ratio—the share of gold and foreign reserves relative to banknotes in circulation—had fallen from 69 to 57 per cent and was rapidly approaching the minimum of 40 per cent required by the gold standard. On 9 October, the government also published new unemployment figures, showing more than 3 million people were out of work. The increase was less rapid than feared, but, nevertheless, the number of jobless kept rising, reaching more than 15 per cent of the total labour force at the end of the year. The situation was particularly dire in the mining, metal, timber, and parts of the textile sectors. In major cities, soup kitchen lines became part of everyday life.[27]

Brüning's situation was further complicated by the activities of the financier Hjalmar Schacht, one of the most controversial figures of the Weimar Republic. Schacht was born into a family of modest wealth. His father was a salesman, first in the United States, then in northern Germany; his mother was of Danish origin and did not bring much of a dowry into the marriage. After a time, his father managed to generate a middle-class income sufficient to finance the studies of his son. Schacht graduated with a degree in economics from the University of Berlin in 1899, joined Dresdner Bank, and became director of the National Bank during the First World War. In 1923, he was named Reich currency commissioner and played a crucial role in ending hyperinflation and organizing monetary reform. Overnight, he became a star, achieving an almost mythical reputation in Germany and elsewhere. As a reward, he was appointed President of the Reichsbank in 1924 and became one of the most influential policymakers in Berlin and on the international stage, especially in Great Britain and the United States. His full name, Hjalmar Horace Greeley Schacht, gave him a cosmopolitan aura, although he was thoroughly German. (Hjalmar was the name given by the Danish grandmother on his mother's side, Horace Greeley was the name of a famous American Republican and abolitionist whom Schacht's liberal father had admired during his years in the United States.)[28]

On the other hand, the man with the pince-nez and the stern look was notorious for his arrogance and wayward tendencies in politics. After the war, he was a co-founder of the left-liberal German Democratic Party (DDP), but then abandoned it in 1926 and gradually moved to the far Right. In January 1933 Hitler would reappoint him as President of the Reichsbank. Schacht was a member of the experts' committee that negotiated the Young Plan in 1929, but then resigned from his post as President of the Reichsbank in early 1930, arguing that the German government had not fought hard enough against the final version of the plan. But he proved incapable of offering a realistic alternative.

Schacht then went to the United States, having received a financially attractive invitation from the Institute of International Education to make no fewer than twenty-eight speeches in October and November, with a fee of $250 per speech. But what really excited him as an ardent patriot was the opportunity to tilt American public opinion in favour of Germany. Of course, some friends warned him about speaking too bluntly. For example, Owen Young wrote to Schacht in mid-August 1930: 'There are many things which a purely private citizen could say in America which . . . you cannot and ought not.' The German government knew about the trip and tried to moderate Schacht. On 1 October 1930, while Schacht was still crossing the Atlantic, Brüning sent him a telegram informing him of the negotiations with Lee, Higginson. Shortly after his arrival in New York, the German Consul General gave a dinner in the roof garden of the St Regis Hotel in order to have an opportunity to talk to Schacht. It was to no avail. Schacht would stick to his script.[29]

Upon arriving in New York on the Hamburg-American liner *Resolute* with his wife and his 20-year-old son Jens who was about to work for First National Bank of Chicago for a year, Schacht gave an extended interview to the American press. The messages of the former head of the Reichsbank were clear and unsettling. 'You must not lay too much stress on the political situation. You should lay more stress on the economic situation. If the German people are going to starve, there are going to be many more Hitlers. You must not think that if you treat a people for ten years as the German people have been treated they will continue to smile. How would you like to be kept in jail for ten years? Tell your people that. Everyone is crying the Germans must be reasonable. I tell you the world must become reasonable. We are.'[30]

Most worryingly, Schacht also expressed his belief that the Young Plan needed to be revised sooner or later. Making such a statement at a time when the German government was in the middle of negotiations with an American bank was likely to be counterproductive. The next day, Schacht was even more blunt, telling an audience in the Astor Hotel that Germany did not have the capacity to pay reparations, that she would be justified in asking immediately for a moratorium on all payments under the Young Plan, and that it was the duty of Chancellor Brüning to give the Allies 'the last chance' to come to terms with Germany in a manner which would enable her to meet her obligations. Brüning reacted immediately, publicly denying that Germany would seek relief from reparation payments. But it had little effect. The American public listened to Schacht and not to the Chancellor, who was hardly known in the USA.[31]

Yet another event threatened to undermine Brüning's plan to end the financial crisis. On Sunday, 5 October 1930, 'Steel Helmet', the right-wing paramilitary organization of former front-line soldiers, gathered in Koblenz on the Rhine, the recently 'liberated' city. The huge rally threw the French public into a state of panic, as two bankers from Lee, Higginson travelling from Paris to Berlin told the German government. This was likely to trigger further withdrawals of French capital from Germany, they argued. French fears were fuelled by Hindenburg's second celebratory trip to the Rhineland on 10 and 11 October, when huge crowds in Aachen and Trier gathered to see the President.[32]

It was at this point that the French side definitively pulled out of negotiations on the foreign loan to Germany. Of course, the French government did not withdraw openly, but signalled to the German attaché in Paris that there were still many issues to be addressed, and the German office understood that the game was over. The reason was as simple as it was clear: the French banks, the Banque de France, and the government were willing to lend, but they could not ignore the fact that public opinion had been unsettled by the Reichstag election results, the Steel Helmet rally, Hindenburg's trip, and other signs of reignited German chauvinism.

A few days later, a German banker who had spoken with the French central bank governor Moreau told Schäffer that the French banks feared that demonstrators would smash their windows if they had participated in the loan. Moreau was also convinced that the Tardieu cabinet would have fallen. 'You cannot imagine how agitated the atmosphere in France has become', he told the German banker.[33]

The French withdrawal was an alarming signal. But, ironically, the deterioration of Franco-German relations helped Berlin to conclude the deal with Lee, Higginson. At 11 p.m. on Saturday evening, 11 October 1930, only one day after the French 'non', the contract was signed. In addition to Lee, Higginson, twenty-two American, one Canadian, three Swedish, twenty-three German, and a consortium of Amsterdam-based German banks participated. The loan amounted to $125 million against a collateral of short-term government bonds of the Reich and was denominated in gold dollars to be protected against potential future German inflation or a devaluation of the Reichsmark. The loan had to be redeemed in three tranches with the final tranche due by November 1932 and bore an effective interest rate of about 6 per cent. At last, Brüning saw light at the end of the tunnel.[34]

Yet, would the Reichstag go along? The first signs were not encouraging. The DVP agitated against its own party member, Foreign Minister Curtius, and demanded a moratorium on the Young Plan. On Saturday, 11 October, Agriculture Minister Martin Schiele stood down from his honorary presidency of the National Rural League, the most important farmers' pressure group, after a heated debate. On Monday, 13 October, the Business Party decided to withdraw its minister from the cabinet, Justice Minister Johann Viktor Bredt. Backed by a public endorsement from President

Hindenburg, Bredt would not budge, but the episode further weakened the Chancellor. Finally, Hugenberg's National People's Party (DNVP) signalled that they would vote against the Brüning cabinet.[35]

On the other hand, there were some powerful supportive trends. Hugenberg's opposition did not have the desired effect. On the contrary, it angered President Hindenburg and made him convinced that he had to reach out to the Social Democrats. It also put more pressure on the Social Democrats. They had to support Brüning if the Weimar Republic was to survive. The party's leading figure was Otto Braun, Minister-President of Prussia, by far the largest Land of the Reich, comprising 60 per cent of Germany's total population. Braun had been heading a coalition of Social Democrats, the left-liberal German Democratic Party, and Brüning's Catholic Centre Party. He was moderate, charismatic, and determined. One day before the Reichstag convened, Hindenburg invited Braun for a conversation. Braun explained that, although he did not have the majority of the party on his side, he would fully support the reform programme. French Foreign Minister Aristide Briand endorsed Braun and directly advised the Social Democrats to support Brüning. And most importantly, the Reichsrat, the chamber of the Länder, adopted the debt redemption law, which was required for obtaining the foreign loan, almost unanimously. Only Thuringia, where a right-wing coalition included the Nazis, abstained.[36]

Still, the opening of the first session of the new Reichstag boded ill for Brüning's plan to end the crisis. Although there was no vote to be taken, the atmosphere was poisoned from the beginning. Both the Communists and National Socialists were wearing their uniforms, even though it was against regulations. When discussing the election of the presidency of the new Reichstag the antagonism between the two radical parties manifested itself almost in a physical fight. The *Vossische Zeitung* reported the scene: 'The battle of words becomes more vibrant. The brownshirts push more and more to the centre of the hall, the Communists march towards them, the opponents are barely separated, throwing hard words at each other—a clash seems imminent.'[37]

What happened outside the Reichstag was even more shocking. The *Vossische Zeitung* spoke of 'unworthy scenes'. Among the many people who gathered outside of the Reichstag, there were quite a few members of the Sturmabteilung (SA), the paramilitary organization of the Nazis, who started to riot in the shopping area nearby. 'Small squads, who were diligently instructed, broke the display windows of particular shops, not randomly, but evidently with a terrorist purpose.' Hitler rapidly tried to reassure the public that no Nazis were involved in these violent acts. The next day, however, the police reported that out of the 108 arrested 45 were members of the Nazi Party and another 55 were sympathizers.[38]

Despite the turmoil, Brüning's informal coalition with the Social Democrats survived the first test. On the second day of the session, the Social Democrat Paul Löbe was re-elected President of the Reichstag by a clear margin of sixty votes. Meanwhile, Otto Braun managed to defend his majority in the Prussian parliament against an extremely militant opposition of the Nazis and the Communists. The day before the vote was taken, Braun was not even able to end his speech because of the rioting of the radical parties in the parliamentary building.[39]

On Saturday, 18 October 1930, the crucial session of the Reichstag took place. After eleven hours of debate the debt redemption bill was decided by a recorded vote that was accompanied by great turmoil. The Nazis repeatedly chorused, 'The Social Democrats have betrayed us.' When they stopped, it was the turn of the

Communists to shout, 'Down with the Social Democrats!' The Nazis then sang the SA song 'Germany, awaken!', while the Communists, punching in the air, struck up 'The Internationale'. The screaming and singing were to no avail. Thanks to the Social Democrats, Brüning won an impressive victory: 325 in favour to 237 against. The foreign loan was secured. The Reichstag also rejected the no-confidence vote by almost the same margin, buried motions aimed at a sudden revision of the Young Plan, and decided to adjourn itself until early December, giving Brüning the required time to enact the austerity programme by invoking Article 48. The Chancellor had prevailed across the board.[40]

'A complete success', State Secretary Pünder wrote in his diary with great relief. His deep pessimism had been proven wrong. Within a month, Brüning ended the currency crisis, restored confidence in Germany's finances, and demonstrated 'that the cabinet and the Reichstag [had] regained the ability to act', as the *Vossische Zeitung* observed with satisfaction. The crushing defeat in the elections had helped to forge an informal grand coalition with the Social Democrats that promised to be an effective formula against the mortal enemies of the Weimar Republic. However, Brüning's victory also constituted a further step away from parliamentary democracy towards an authoritarian form of government. The adjournment of the Reichstag meant that the executive branch became more powerful. After the October session, the Reichstag would never reconvene again without the will of the cabinet.[41]

6

'THE FIRST REAL CHANCELLOR SINCE BISMARCK'

Investors reacted euphorically to Brüning's victory. 'The Government's success in the Reichstag on Saturday has immediately put new heart into the Stock Exchange', *The Times* reported from Berlin. Within two weeks the Young Plan bond climbed 5 per cent, and the Reichsbank's gold and foreign exchange reserves returned to comfortable levels, as capital was streaming back to Germany. The stability of the Reichsmark was secured for the time being.[1]

It was not a return to normality, however. Only the immediate panic disappeared; the fear of another drop of confidence due to political disturbances was ever present. For this reason, the Reichsbank continued to keep the official interest rate at the high level of 5 per cent, while the Bank of England, the Banque de France, and the New York Fed had their rates between 2 and 3 per cent. More importantly, Chancellor Brüning was condemned to continue his austerity policies. Fulfilling the conditions of the Young Plan required that Germany achieve both a fiscal and a trade surplus in an environment of recession and falling prices. The fiscal surplus was needed to provide the funds for reparations; the trade surplus obtained the foreign exchange reserves necessary to make the transfers to the creditor countries.

Obtaining another foreign loan would have lessened these restrictions. But given Germany's unstable political situation, there was little reason to believe that Lee, Higginson or any another bank would be willing to come up with a new offer. Another option that might loosen the straitjacket would be to declare a moratorium on reparation payments. The Young Plan explicitly allowed for such a procedure. But even if the moratorium was declared in a legally correct way by invoking the Special Advisory Committee of the Bank for International Settlements (BIS), a financial crisis would ensue. Investors would bet on a German default. Brüning clearly saw that this clause was counterproductive. 'Calling on the Special Advisory Committee would shatter our credit in the most severe way', he explained in a cabinet meeting.[2]

On the other hand, if Brüning continued to fulfil the Young Plan by imposing one austerity package after another, the crisis would become ever deeper and the opposition ever stronger. Hitler was relentlessly attacking the Weimar establishment, not only in the Nazi press but, since the elections, also in the foreign press. At the end of September, he was invited to write an opinion column for the *Sunday Express*, one of the most popular British newspapers, owned by the 'Baron of Fleet Street', Lord Beaverbrook. In the first paragraphs, Hitler diligently played the far-sighted German statesman who was bound to protect the free world:

> Let not the world deceive itself. Germany will either have to become a free nation again or, losing faith in any other future, be driven into the beckoning arms of Bolshevism.
>
> That is no mere phrase, nor threat nor prophecy, but just a statement of fact and of the sentiment of the German masses today. I know that sentiment as no other statesman or politician does in Berlin.
>
> The choice—between freedom and the right to live, and Bolshevism—lies less with the German people than with those who

have laid down the impossible conditions, an unbearable burden on Germany for generations to come.

If you deliberately drive a people into poverty, their transformation into a political proletariat is bound to follow. That is what is taking place in Germany today.

The German election of September 14 is a warning. It tore away the veil, and partly revealed the soul of Germany.

He then criticized the Versailles Treaty and the Young Plan and presented the Nazis as the only honest party that defended the legitimate interests of the German people:

Promise upon promise has been made to the patient, industrious, hard-working, order-loving German people. Every year conditions have grown worse, every year the burden has become heavier, the suffering greater, and the future darker. Our people have lost faith in promises and those who make them. Their confidence in the old political leaders and parties has gone. If the German people should definitively lose their faith in a future of their own choice, then the gravest developments are inevitable.

The National Socialist Party has been born out of the sufferings of the German nation. Our aim, our purpose, is to free Germany from political and economic conditions that mean enslavement; from burdens as unjust as they are impossible, burdens that no nation, no people can carry for generation after generation…Neither I nor the National Socialist Party is a danger in Germany. The danger is those German statesmen, those political parties, and those newspapers who mislead us at home and abroad as to the feeling welling up in the German masses.

His commentary ended with another warning to the creditor nations and a thinly disguised invitation to support his party:

Europe is passing through one of the gravest crises in its history. The Versailles Treaty and the Young Plan are the axis around which much will revolve in the next few years. You cannot ruin and Bolshevise Germany and think that the rest of Europe will remain immune. That is blindness. The German people are not resigned apathetically to the tragic fate that their enemies, knowingly or unknowingly, are forcing on them. Thank God, they are not resigned. They have a spirit of determination and will. United and properly directed, they will survive, and will benefit the world. My confidence in the German people is unlimited. My aim is their freedom. That is my mission.[3]

Not only the Nazis but also the federation of Social Democratic labour unions openly advocated a revision of the Young Plan. In October 1930, the federation released a statement that left no doubt about its position: 'It is certain that the billions which Germany has to pay its creditors are not only one of the causes of the enormous unemployment in Germany, but also of the disturbances in the global economy. It is therefore a dictate of economic reason and statesmanship to eliminate these obstacles to a sound development of the global economy.'[4]

Brüning was trapped and besieged. His only hope was that the creditor countries would realize how serious the situation in Germany had become and negotiate a new agreement. But was such a hope realistic?

In France, there were indeed voices on the Left demanding closer cooperation with Germany, after the election results became known. But they constituted only a small minority. The general sense was that Germany did not need any help; it just had to put its finances in order. One reason for this uncompromising attitude was that the French themselves had yet to feel the effects of the depression and didn't really understand what Germany was going through. In addition, many in France were afraid of a revanchist Germany that supposedly was preparing for another war. Helping them would only strengthen the reactionary forces.[5]

In accord with the general mood, *Le Temps*, the pro-government newspaper, sent a clear warning across the Rhine. Hitler's victory in the elections demanded 'prudence, vigilance, and firmness', it wrote. 'Germany is not to make any mistakes, nor is Europe.' The right-wing French press was even more critical. *Le Figaro* said that the results of the German elections showed that French appeasement had completely failed: 'The German elections have only one meaning: revenge; in other words, war.' It argued: 'There is no example in history of a great nation that, having lost a long-held military hegemony, does not use all its forces to reclaim this domination. Germany is not reacting differently from France after 1815.'[6]

Accordingly, the French government had little leeway, regardless of whether it wanted to help Brüning or not. The only thing Briand and Tardieu could offer was a long-term loan to Germany in exchange for political concessions. A first initiative was launched on 19 September 1930, four days after the elections, at the Council of the League of Nations in Geneva. Briand restated his position in a conversation with German Foreign Minister Curtius. The French government would not agree to a revision of the Young Plan so soon after the conference at The Hague and the evacuation of the Rhineland, but invited the Germans to begin talks about a French long-term loan. Predictably, the Germans were not interested. Some German newspapers even warned against the 'loan danger', suspecting that France was trying to tie Germany's hands in order to avoid a revision of the Young Plan. Even the internationalist Hans Schäffer was sceptical of Briand's loan proposal. 'Not now', he wrote in his diary.[7]

After the failure of Briand's initiative, Franco-German negotiations came to a complete halt because of the collapse of the Tardieu cabinet. The immediate reason for Tardieu's fall was the so-called Oustric affair, named after a French entrepreneur and banker. Albert Oustric specialized in restructuring companies and invested on behalf of his clients, among them many small depositors, in many different industries. In October 1930, his highly leveraged conglomerate was faltering as a result of the failure of some of the companies in which it held stakes. Many small savers were ruined and felt defrauded. Tardieu himself had not been involved in any wrongdoing, but his Minister of Justice, Raoul Péret, had obstructed the indictment of Oustric. On 21 November, the Chamber of Deputies appointed a commission of inquiry to investigate the political connections in the affair. Tardieu resigned after losing a vote in the Senate on 4 December. Evidently, not only the opposition, but also some of his initial supporters, had got tired of his abrasive, authoritarian style.[8]

Tardieu's fall opened a period of several weeks during which no stable government could be formed. President Gaston Doumergue first called on Louis Barthou, an independent with centrist ideas, to try to put together a majority for a new cabinet. He failed. Doumergue then asked Pierre Laval, an independent and former Minister of Labour in the Tardieu cabinet. Again, no working majority could be found. Théodore Steeg became Prime Minister in mid-December, but his government collapsed after a few weeks. Finally, in late January 1931, Laval tried once more and managed to assemble a stable cabinet which was more or less a reshuffle of the old one. Tardieu became Minister of Agriculture, and Briand and Maginot held on to their positions as Minister for Foreign Affairs and Minister of War respectively. Now, the French were open to negotiations with Germany again, but three valuable months had been wasted.

The British press showed more understanding than the French of the German situation. Nevertheless, most commentators saw no need for debt relief, expecting that Germany would have the capacity to overcome the crisis. *The Times* believed that 'it would be a mistake to put too sinister an interpretation upon what after all may only prove to be a very transitory phase of German politics. The fact remains that in the new Reichstag, no less than in the last, the orderly and stable elements of democratic government are still largely preponderant.' *The Economist*, though clearly identifying the vicious circle of reparations, economic crisis, and political radicalization, saw no reason for panic. The editorial pointed to 'a number of features in the situation which may mitigate our anxiety'. Prussia, which covered two-thirds of Germany, was in the hands of the Social Democrats, there was a chance that the success would sober the extremists, and there was the personality and prestige of President von Hindenburg, whom it described as 'one other solid rock in Germany's political foundations'. Only one prominent voice went against the consensus. Lord Rothermere, owner of the *Daily Mail*, welcomed the victory of the Nazis seeing them as a bulwark against Bolshevism. But this was no great help to Brüning. On the contrary, by portraying him as a transitory figure, the Rothermere press made his position even weaker than it already was.[9]

Given the state of British public opinion towards Germany, Prime Minister Ramsay MacDonald was in no position to make an offer to Brüning. More importantly, he was himself heading a minority cabinet that had to deal with the deepening economic crisis and strained government finances. Consequently, when the British ambassador in Berlin, Sir Horace Rumbold, cabled to London that Foreign Minister Julius Curtius was airing the idea of a debt moratorium, the British reaction was harsh. British Foreign Secretary Henderson wrote back to Rumbold that 'the existing financial and economic position of Germany does not in any way justify the German Government in suggesting that it may be necessary to declare a moratorium'. His main argument was that 'the economic difficulties from which Germany in common with the rest of the world is suffering are not such as to necessitate any postponement of transfers or reopening of The Hague settlement'. On 10 December 1930 Rumbold went to Curtius to read to him the whole dispatch. Berlin could expect nothing from London.[10]

The American press took a similar approach. The *New York Times* warned of exaggerated pessimism: 'Today the indicated Republican majority is half that of 1924, but still sufficient to organize a Government if the coalition of Socialists and middle parties is re-established. Efforts to that end were under way before the election, plainly in anticipation of its results. Events would seem to compel a renewal of the partnership of moderate elements under whose guidance Germany has won back strength and prestige.' *The Times* published an article which reiterated the positive assessment expressed by influential Wall Street figures: 'Bankers who are informed about German political and economic affairs asserted yesterday that they saw no cause for concern in the results of the Reichstag elections.'[11]

In Washington, the idea of reducing or cancelling war debts claims on the former allies, France and Great Britain, was simply taboo. President Hoover was in a weak position. His prediction in early March that the slump would be over within thirty or sixty days had proved overly optimistic, to say the least. By October, industrial production had declined by another 20 per cent (Fig. 6.1). Stock prices had plummeted by a third since their peak in mid-April. In addition, a severe drought was devastating the Great Plains, the heart of US agriculture. The morale of the American people was at a record low. Hoover's party would be severely punished by voters in the congressional mid-term elections on 4 November. The

Fig. 6.1 Index of US industrial production (1929 = 100)

Republicans lost the majority in the House by one vote (217 to 218) and could secure only a slim majority in the Senate (48 to 47). And the economic crisis continued to drag on. Industrial production kept declining, the unemployment rate was climbing to 10 per cent, and hundreds of banks failed.[12]

Only two yellow press papers, the *New York World* of the Pulitzer group and the *New York American* of the Hearst group, demanded an end to German reparation payments. But they had no impact on the Hoover administration. Likewise, the meetings of Hjalmar Schacht, the former president of the Reichsbank, with Hoover and the Secretary of State Henry Stimson came to nothing. After the meeting with Schacht, Stimson rushed to reassure French ambassador Paul Claudel, the famous writer and brother of the sculptor Camille Claudel: 'I told him of Dr. Schacht's visit to me in the Department and how I had come to then ask him to lunch at my house on Sunday. I told him that on neither of these occasions had any propositions been brought forward by Dr. Schacht regarding the political or business situation in Germany nor had such situation been discussed—that both meetings were purely personal and social . . .'[13]

Thus, Brüning had little reason to hope that the creditor countries would be open to a new agreement. There was no rallying cry in London, Paris, or Washington to liberate Germany from its debt trap. Diplomats agreed that the Young Plan could not be revised less than a year after the Hague conference, and politicians tried to gain time believing that an economic recovery would ultimately solve all problems. The rhythms of the economic crisis and of international politics were out of sync.

While diplomats and politicians continued to be complacent, some independent observers, including Felix Somary, were becoming increasingly frightened by the course of events. But to the dismay of many in the banking community, he largely withdrew from public appearances after his January speeches in Heidelberg and Berlin. In April, he married Countess May Demblin de Ville who had joined Blankart & Cie. in 1929 as an executive assistant. After the wedding in Salzburg, the couple went to Sorrento and enjoyed an extended honeymoon in Italy.

However, when he received an invitation from the prestigious Royal Institute of International Affairs in London to make a speech there in December, he seized it. He first laid out the reasons for the economic crisis and then discussed its political implications. His main message was that fear of communism spreading across the European continent was unfounded, but that another war was becoming increasingly probable. 'We are rapidly approaching a *turning-point* in European affairs. If an *entente* between Italy and Germany were to replace the Briand–Stresemann epoch, it would be difficult to avoid war. The rise of the Hitler party was a direct consequence of the crisis, which drove large masses of a ruined people into the arms of the most radical of the Nationalist leaders.'

As for remedies to end the crisis, he urged his listeners to abandon their complacency. 'Some people expect that the crisis will be solved by the US reducing tariffs and forgiving European debts. I am quite sure that this is inevitable, but I am by no means certain that it will come about at the right time. What is needed is immediate action.' To Somary, there were only two measures that would alter the situation radically. The first was a readjustment of the international price structure: prices of finished goods had to be lowered, those of raw materials increased. This readjustment would allow the periphery to gain more purchasing power and the rich countries to increase their exports. Somary was thinking of temporary government purchases of raw materials to revive demand and destroy numerous cartels and syndicates, 'those parasites of our economic life', and a lowering of industrial wages to enable cuts in the prices of finished goods.

His second idea was to take steps to reduce the imbalance between France and Germany in the hope of restoring political confidence in Europe. 'As long as France hoards and Germany invests her savings outside her own borders, a recovery on the Continent is impossible. Europa has no lack of capital; what she needs is confidence. I am convinced that France and Germany, working separately, will not find a way out; England must bring them together a second time. If Great Britain has neither the will nor the strength to do so, then the present crisis will be but a prelude to a dark period to which the historian of the future will give the name "Between Two Wars".'

Interestingly, when the floor was opened to questions, most people asked about his first proposal, that is: the readjustment of prices of raw materials and finished goods. Only one question focused on the plan to bring France and Germany together. Somary responded by repeating the urgency of action: 'The political side of the situation is a very serious one. I have noticed with interest and pleasure that some of my remarks have been taken lightly by a London audience; but in all my life I have not seen so dangerous a situation as the present.' Somary ended his presentation by appealing once more to the responsibility of the English political elite: 'England is the one natural leader of the Continent and cannot be replaced by any other country. If political confidence were restored, the crisis would only be an episode; if not, it would be the first act of a tragedy.'[14]

Following up on his pessimistic analysis, Somary withdrew all the funds that his bank had on deposit with banks in England, Germany, and Italy in the early months of 1931. His partners at Blankart & Cie. resisted the move, thinking that his pessimism was exaggerated and would be destructive for the business. Somary went ahead anyway.[15]

Seeing that foreign governments were not ready to help him despite the alarming election results, Brüning began to think about a more aggressive foreign policy. In mid-December, he summoned his inner circle and shared with them his view that domestic politics would force the government to take action on the reparations front, probably before the end of February 1931. Curtius, Dietrich, and Luther agreed, but they saw no possibility of making progress without causing a dangerous disruption. Luther then came up with a new idea: 'Could we not thrust the guidance again into the hands of America, maybe by way of disarmament?'[16] Brüning and Curtius liked the proposal, and the group agreed on linking a debt moratorium to 'a really big, comprehensive political action'.[17]

Four days later, Brüning had a meeting with US ambassador Frederic Sackett (Illustration 11). The idea for a personal conversation came from Sackett who was seeking a larger role in Berlin.

Illustration 11. US ambassador Frederick Sackett and his wife Olive Speed Sackett in Berlin.

The former businessman and Republican senator from Kentucky, who became ambassador to Germany thanks to his friendship with Hoover, loved the spotlight. He turned the American embassy into a hotspot of Berlin's social life. His wife Olive, the daughter of a wealthy Kentucky businessman who had made his money in coal mining and the manufacture of cement, was in charge of organizing the parties.[18]

Bella Fromm, a then famous chronicler of Berlin's high society, was impressed: 'Went to the station to meet the new American Ambassador, Frederic M. Sackett. A gentle-looking man with, obviously, very good background. Mrs. Sackett is an attractive woman of great distinction.' After an evening at Sackett's house she wrote: 'The American Ambassador and his wife are showing people here what "entertaining" means. Even the international diplomats are stunned. The Sacketts serve lobster at tea, an unheard-of luxury in Berlin! The Ambassador has rented a small but aristocratic palace in the most fashionable quarter of Berlin. A gigantic and aged butler commands a small army of footmen in discreet blue livery. Mrs. Olive Sackett-Speed is the astonishing possessor of a social secretary, an extravagant novelty here. She is a perfect hostess and gathers as many pre-war courtiers to her house as possible.'[19]

For Brüning, the conversation with the American ambassador came at the right time, giving him a perfect opportunity to present his new initiative. He was confident that Sackett would take the bait, believing that he was politically naive and easy to manipulate. And, in fact, the ambassador immediately liked Brüning's idea of an all-encompassing conference and promised to write a private letter to President Hoover.[20]

The timing for the initiative was good. In Washington the consensus on inter-allied war debts and German reparations was slowly shifting. In mid-December 1930, Secretary of State Henry Stimson had had a meeting with his closest associate, Undersecretary Joseph Cotton, about Germany's dire economic prospects. Stimson was convinced that the United States had to do something to prevent a looming catastrophe in Europe from spilling over to the American economy. In late December 1930, Stimson also talked to President Hoover. Both agreed that Germany was seeking a reduction of reparations in a fair way, 'because she had been making a very honest attempt to get along this winter on her own resources and that she was putting through a program of retrenchment which really cut to the bone'. The President, an early critic of the Versailles Treaty, had a clear grasp of the problems in Europe.[21]

Not only Hoover and his confidants, but also influential people outside the White House, began to question the conventional view. Albert Wiggin, Chairman of the Board of the Chase Bank, publicly wrote in the bank's annual report that the United States should cut a portion of European war debts: 'Cancellation or reduction of the inter-allied debts has been increasingly discussed throughout the world. This question has an importance far beyond the dollar magnitude of the debts involved. Without commenting on the many arguments on both sides of the controversy and aside from the question of the justice of cancellation, I am firmly convinced it would be good business for our government to initiate a reduction in these debts at this time.'[22] Wiggin was backed by Sir Herbert Holt, head of the Royal Bank of Canada.[23] And even Owen D. Young, the architect of the Young Plan, told Hoover that reparations and debts should be reduced by 20 per cent.[24]

In January 1931, Secretary Stimson took the initiative by instructing the energetic Undersecretary Cotton to go to Europe to prepare the ground for an economic conference. The former Harvard-trained lawyer, who had worked with President Hoover in the food administration during the war, was a good choice. He had distinguished himself as acting Secretary of State in Washington while Stimson was participating in the London Naval Conference in the spring of 1930, and early on he developed an understanding of the difficult situation of Germany. There was a real chance that Cotton would be able to create momentum in international financial diplomacy.

Yet, while arranging his travel to Europe, Cotton fell sick. He was taken to Johns Hopkins Hospital in Baltimore where he was diagnosed with an infection of the spinal cord. On 21 January, surgeons removed a tumour from his spine, but Cotton never recovered from this operation and eventually died. His mission had to be cancelled, and Hoover, though listening to people like Wiggin or Owen, decided not to pursue the matter further. On 2 February, Ambassador Sackett had to report to the German Foreign Ministry that nothing had come of his initiative in Washington.[25]

Sackett did not give up, however. He was convinced that Washington was the only power that had the capacity to cut a new deal between the creditors and the German government. He gathered statistical evidence showing how reparations negatively affected Germany's balance of payments and public finances and sent it to the Federal Reserve Bank of New York, hoping that it would prompt American officials to act. Sackett was also encouraged by a new initiative from the French side. On 6 February 1931, the French writer and diplomat Wladimir d'Ormesson published a proposal that linked a temporary reduction of reparations to arms limitation. According to his plan, Germany would pay only half of the unconditioned annuities from 1931 to 1933, provided that the United States renounced 50 per cent of the payments from France. In addition, France and Germany would cut their military budgets by one-twelfth. Brüning reacted positively, although he was seeking more than temporary relief.[26]

On 9 February 1931, Aristide Briand supported the participation of French banks in another loan to Germany that was orchestrated by Lee, Higginson. It was not a big deal, as it only served to pre-finance the sale of Reichsbahn preferential shares by the German government to the Reich Insurance Institute for Employees. Nevertheless, it sent a positive message. The *Vossische Zeitung* considered it 'one of those small peace doves that, for the first time since 14 September, circulate between Berlin and the French capital'. The *New York Times* reported from Paris that 'bankers here yesterday expressed gratification that French bankers participated, since it marks the first time since the war that France has lent money directly to the German Government'.[27]

At the same time, investors were turning bullish. From the beginning of January to the end of February 1931, the Dow Jones Industrial Average jumped from 160 to 190 points. In mid-January 1931, Albert H. Wiggin observed that 'we are approximately at the worst of the depression', and predicted that 'conditions at the end of 1931 will be better than at the end of 1930'. The Young Plan bond recovered from around 70 in early January to almost 80 in mid-March, thus returning to the level before the Reichstag elections held in September 1930. Perhaps the much-hoped-for recovery was finally taking hold.[28]

Furthermore, Brüning was strengthening his position on the domestic front. On 7 February 1931, a sound majority of the

Reichstag rejected the no-confidence votes initiated by the radical parties. On 10 February, the Communists, Hugenberg's National People's Party (DNVP), and the Nazis quit the session when the Reichstag adopted new parliamentary standing orders that punished verbal insults during the debate, excluded obstruction tactics, and gave committees more importance at the expense of the plenary sessions. As only the Communists returned to the next session, Foreign Minister Curtius easily survived another no-confidence vote. British ambassador Rumbold was full of admiration: 'The large majorities obtained by Dr Brüning in the opening days of the present session in the Reichstag again impressed public opinion with his qualities of leadership, and showed that the other political parties had at last realized the necessity of standing up to the extremists. An acquaintance of mine from East Prussia, who is a German Nationalist by conviction, recently informed me that Herr von Oldenburg-Januschau, who is the incarnation of Prussian Junkerdom and has sat in the Reichstag for over forty years, had expressed to him the view that Dr Brüning was the first real Chancellor Germany had had since the days of Bismarck.'[29]

The growing recognition of Brüning's success and the fear that a failure of his cabinet would bring about a collapse of the Weimar Republic finally led the British government to make an important gesture. As in Washington, the consensus in London had begun to shift over the course of the winter. In mid-January, Sir Josiah Stamp, a director of the Bank of England and a negotiator of the Young Plan, told the *Daily Telegraph* 'that the burden on Germany under the Young plan had become much greater than had been intended'. Likewise, Sir Frederick Leith-Ross, a senior Treasury official, signalled that he would be open to a revision of the Young Plan.[30]

Again, it was Ambassador Sackett who came up with the idea of a British initiative. At a dinner with British ambassador Rumbold in early March 1931, he showed himself convinced that '[a] gesture on the part of England would do more for the Brüning Government than anything else'. The Danish ambassador in Berlin also reminded Rumbold that 'England and France should do something to help the Brüning Government.' A few days later, Rumbold sent a cable to London in which he proposed inviting Brüning to Chequers, the Prime Minister's official country retreat. 'I repeat again that Brüning's prestige is great in Germany, and the way in which he has faced up to his country's difficulties has, I think, impressed public opinion in other countries, but he does not, like Curtius, know any of the leading statesmen of Europe, and a visit to England would, I think, give him an international prestige which would be helpful to him in Germany itself. I cannot imagine anything which would more impress and please the Germans than if he were to spend a week-end at Chequers, for instance.'[31]

The German government received the invitation on 24 March and made it public on 8 April. It was the first time since the war that German ministers had been invited to Great Britain other than to attend an official conference. True, the British side only wanted to talk about the question of disarmament, but it opened the possibility of talking about the economic situation and the reparations as well.[32]

Was the time ripe for a grand bargain among Britain, France, and Germany? There were still great obstacles to overcome. Most importantly, the Franco-German relationship continued to be difficult. Theoretically, many French and German politicians wanted to strengthen cooperation, but in practice they were afraid of taking the required steps. When the French Chamber of Deputies debated the loan to the German government in February 1931, there were many critical voices who feared that Germany would use these funds for rearmament.[33]

A particularly astute analyst of Franco-German relations was the 66-year-old Marcus Wallenberg Sr, a scion of the renowned Swedish family. Wallenberg had been Chief Executive Officer of Stockholms Enskilda Bank, the bedrock of the Wallenberg business empire, before launching himself into a career in international financial diplomacy in the 1920s. He was involved in the implementation of the Dawes Plan and the Young Plan and travelled regularly across Europe. He had friends everywhere. One of them was State Secretary Hans Schäffer in Berlin. In late February 1931, he told Schäffer after a trip to Paris: 'The French, even the right-leaning ones, are very strongly in favour of a rapprochement with Germany. They speak a great deal about economic cooperation. Yet, as soon as one enters a discussion about concrete plans, one gets the general response, even from left-leaning men, that they could not make any far-reaching concessions because of public opinion in Paris.'[34]

Similarly, the German ambassador in Paris, von Hoesch, wrote in early March: 'Each Franco-German debate between those who seek understanding follows a similar pattern. First, one talks about political issues and the conclusion is reached that they are insoluble and that the German claims can only be accepted with great restrictions. Then one proceeds to the question of economic and financial cooperation... At first, the idea of a general economic association between the two countries drums up enthusiasm... But this discussion does not lead to any practical results... When asked what needs to be done to convince the French public to make long-term investments in Germany, the widely shared answer is that in a first step, "trust" has be created. When discussing the question of how trust could be created, one gets the answer that trust requires a comprehensive political settlement at which point one returns again to the starting point of the conversation.'[35]

PART III

DESPAIR

7

SQUARING THE CIRCLE

The period of indecision came to a close on Friday, 6 March. Late in the afternoon, the Chancellor was informed by agitated senior officials of the Finance Ministry that the Reich's revenues were deteriorating rapidly. 'Brutal measures will be unavoidable', Finance Minister Dietrich warned. Reichsbank President Luther, who also attended the emergency meeting, confirmed the depressing outlook. Brüning listened attentively, explained that he understood their concerns, and then drew a far-reaching conclusion: 'The German people will not tolerate another compression in our finances without decisive steps on reparations. I am therefore determined to act.'[1]

Luther and Hans Schäffer, State Secretary of the Finance Ministry, were aghast. They were convinced that questioning Germany's obligation to fulfil the Young Plan would immediately trigger a financial crisis. Investors would begin to doubt the solvency of the Reich, provoking massive capital flight. By contrast, Hermann Pünder, ever the loyal State Secretary of the Chancellery, embraced the new policy wholeheartedly. Three days after the historic meeting he wrote in his diary: 'Continuing to cut back, without reform of reparations, is breaking the spirit of our impoverished people.'[2]

Who was right? Would a more aggressive foreign policy improve the domestic standing of the government? Was there a way to achieve a revision of the Young Plan without provoking a major diplomatic and financial crisis?

The Chancellor soon received a first answer to these questions. On 16 March, Foreign Minister Curtius informed the cabinet that he had been negotiating secretly with Austria with a view to establishing a customs union. Two days later, the cabinet supported the idea unanimously. Curtius knew that Brüning saw a more muscular foreign policy as a way to counter the government's low approval rate. 'This step promises to have a de-stressing effect on domestic politics', Curtius explained with great confidence. 'We may even get a united front of the Social Democrats and the National Socialists around this issue.' The economic effects of the customs union were considered secondary by Curtius. Austria was too small a market to fuel German exports in a decisive way.[3]

However, the gambit failed completely. When the French Foreign Ministry was officially notified three days later, the reaction could not have been more hostile. 'Our plan has aroused great dismay and indignation', the German ambassador cabled from Paris to Berlin. French Foreign Minister Briand, usually good-tempered and measured in tone, shouted: 'This is a preparation for the Anschluss!' Soon the German term was in everybody's mouth, and the name Curtius, until recently hardly known to anybody outside the Reich, became a symbol for arrogance.[4]

The pro-government newspaper *Le Temps* went even further than Briand. It considered the plan to be 'an attempt to realize the old project of "Mittel-Europa" by which Germany would have sought to establish her domination if she had emerged from the war victorious'. In the parliamentary debate that followed a few days later, Briand once more lashed out against the German government. 'The Austro-German agreement obviously marks the moment to call a halt in our relations with Germany', he thundered. 'Precautions will need to be taken.' The French Foreign Minister had every reason to be furious. Only a few weeks earlier he had indignantly downplayed the danger of an Anschluss during a parliamentary debate. He had been well and truly duped.[5]

Briand argued that Austria was violating the peace treaties of 1919 and the Geneva Protocol of 1922. Article 88 of the Treaty of Saint-Germain stipulated: 'The independence of Austria is inalienable otherwise than with the consent of the Council of the League of Nations.' This was linked to Article 80 of the Treaty of Versailles (1919): 'Germany acknowledges and will respect strictly the independence of Austria within the frontiers which may be fixed in a treaty between that State and the principal allied and associated powers; she agrees that this independence shall be inalienable except with the consent of the Council of the League of Nations.' The Geneva Protocol of 1922, which settled the conditions for the stabilization loan Austria obtained from the League of Nations, stipulated that Austria would 'abstain from every economic or financial negotiation and engagement which might be of a nature to directly or indirectly compromise this independence'. Briand also criticized Germany for supposedly violating the most-favoured nation clause in its trade agreements with Britain and France of 1924 and 1927 respectively. If Germany granted lower customs tariffs in a new treaty, it was obliged to harmonize the existing treaties with the new one.[6]

Whether nor not the French arguments were legally watertight was irrelevant. In fact, there was even a good chance that they were not. What really mattered was the political dimension, and in this respect Curtius's move undoubtedly was a blunder. From this moment on, France would be even more reluctant to seek closer cooperation with Germany. The Paris correspondent of *The Times* wrote that 'it is certain that those who have been most active in promoting a Franco-German rapprochement are much disturbed and disappointed by what has happened'. And Paris was not alone in its criticism. The Czechs and the Italians soon joined the French chorus, followed by most other European governments. Even the British, after some restraint in the first days after the news broke, took a critical stance. On 25 March, the British ambassador, Sir Horace Rumbold, visited Brüning to read him a telegram that explained the misgivings of the British Foreign Office. Only some US officials reacted positively. 'It is a wise thing for them to do', Senator Borah, the influential chairman of the Senate Foreign Relations Committee, declared. 'Europe cannot recover until there is a great change in the spirit of the Versailles Treaty. I cannot see how anyone in Europe can object to the arrangement.' But in European affairs of the time, Washington was much less important than London and Paris.[7]

Of course, Curtius had expected some resistance. When seeking the approval of the cabinet, he conceded that the political risks created by his plan were 'considerable'. Still, he seemed to have completely underestimated the rage of French politicians. He believed that they would accept the plan after studying the formal details. Having the mind of a lawyer who was used to a rule-based approach to any problem, he lacked a feel for the vagaries of politics and the ambiguities of diplomacy. The British Permanent Undersecretary of State for Foreign Affairs, Sir Robert Vansittart, observed wryly that Curtius was 'dying to connect his name with something'.[8]

More importantly, however, the idea of forming a customs union did not make any sense economically. Austria was a small country of only 6.7 million inhabitants, less than a tenth of Germany's population. Its economy was weak, with a GDP per capita 10 per cent lower than Germany's. It was hard to see how a reduction of tariffs between the two countries would have provided much of a boost to the German exporting sectors. Conversely, Austria did not have any natural resources that were of special use for German industry. Curtius himself conceded that in economic terms Austria surely would have 'the bigger advantage for the time being'.[9]

Remarkably, in the crucial meeting on 18 March, Brüning did not stop his Foreign Minister. In his memoirs, he reports that he was not supportive, but does not answer the question why he did not veto the plan. In any case, he had been warned.[10]

Surprisingly, the customs union project, although making Franco-German relations even more difficult than they already were, did not unsettle financial markets. The price of the Young Plan bond hardly moved, neither did the exchange rate of the Reichsmark. Optimistic American investors even considered the Austro-German customs union a first step towards a more liberal trade order in Europe. A press release from National City Bank in New York stated that 'as a business proposition it seems like a stroke of practical statesmanship'. And since the Austrian and German governments agreed in mid-April to seek the approval of the League of Nations, most investors believed that tensions would cool.[11]

What was more, Germany's economic outlook continued to improve. In early April 1931, the leading economic magazine, *Der deutsche Volkswirt*, wrote that the 'positive trend of the stock exchange shows that despite there being few signs of recovery, investors believe that the nadir of the crisis has been reached'. Industrial production was climbing back to the levels of autumn 1930. And thanks to growing confidence, the Reichsbank was accumulating foreign exchange reserves. Some observers even expected a reduction of the central bank rate in the coming weeks. US ambassador Sackett sent an optimistic note to the Federal Reserve Bank of New York: 'I have the distinct impression that things are looking better in Germany.' To Sackett there was no doubt that 'a very considerable amount of German money which fled abroad is returning here'.[12]

On the domestic political front, things looked even better. Brüning went from success to success. On 20 March, the Reichstag approved the third tranche for the pocket battleship A and the first tranche for the pocket battleship B, securing broader support for Brüning in bourgeois and nationalist milieus. (Pocket battle-ships were small, heavily armed cruisers specially built to conform with the limitations of tonnage and armament imposed by the Treaty of Versailles.) On 25 March, the Reichstag passed the budget for the new fiscal year and agreed not to reconvene until October of 1931. This was a sensational victory for Brüning. The *Vossische Zeitung* was enthusiastic: 'We can have confidence in the future again, we can dare to hope again.' On 28 March, an emergency decree banning paramilitary uniforms, side arms, and propaganda trucks and forbidding political demonstrations not approved by the authorities was signed by President Hindenburg. This support from the head of state made Brüning more credible among Liberals and Social Democrats who were increasingly frightened by rising civil disorder. In the year up to March 1931, about 300 people had died in street clashes between the Communists and the Nazis. Encouraged by the turn of events, Pünder wrote in his diary: 'In domestic politics we have come through a period of great successes. We have shown to the entire public at home and abroad that this cabinet can impose its will on parliament.'[13]

Even more encouraging for the Chancellor, the National Socialists were facing significant setbacks. On 1 April, a majority in the parliament of Thuringia passed a no-confidence vote brought by the Social Democrats and aimed at removing the Nazi ministers Wilhelm Frick and Willy Marschler from the government. Frick, one of Hitler's closest collaborators for more than ten years, had been the first Nazi to hold a ministerial-level post in the Weimar Republic. In January 1930, he had become Minister for the Interior and Education in a right-wing coalition government in Thuringia. No sooner had he been appointed than he began to purge schools and agencies of Communists and Social Democrats and promote the hiring of Nazis in the police corps. He also banned newspapers, censored the novel and the film *All Quiet on the Western Front*, a critical account of the life of German soldiers in the trenches, and forced the University of Jena to appoint a social anthropologist who held eugenicist ideas. After little more than a year, Frick's aggressive policies annoyed another member of the coalition, the German People's Party, and many of its members happily endorsed the Social Democrats' no-confidence vote.

The Nazi Party was also weakened by a struggle between the Sturmabteilung (SA) and Hitler. Walther Stennes, the head of the SA in north-eastern Germany, wanted to take to the streets to protest Brüning's recent emergency measures against radical parties, while Hitler insisted on maintaining a policy of legality. As Stennes would not budge, Hitler removed him on 31 March from his post in Berlin and ordered him to take a position in the party headquarters in Munich. In retaliation, Stennes sent his loyal troops to occupy the SA agency and the editorial office of the Nazi weekly *Der Angriff* in Berlin. Joseph Goebbels, the district leader of Berlin, who was in Munich to be with Hitler, was shattered: 'This is the most serious crisis that the party has had to face.' Hitler and Goebbels fought back, expelled Stennes from the party, and called in the Berlin police to help retake control of the occupied offices. Stennes still would not retreat and fired up his Berlin stormtroopers to revolt openly against Hitler. Only after another intervention by the party leadership did the Stennes revolt collapse. On 4 April, Goebbels, exhausted from the confrontation, wrote in his diary: 'Yesterday was a gruesome Good Friday. My critical hour. But I think it is over.'[14]

Yet, as expected by the Chancellor and the Finance Ministry, the fiscal situation had become unsustainable. The economic recovery was too weak and only temporary. In the second quarter, industrial production resumed its downward path (Fig. 7.1). And even though the number of unemployed was decreasing due to seasonal factors, poverty was spreading. Jobless parents and their families depending on shrinking communal welfare subsidies often went hungry. In June 1931, the German Medical Association warned that 'the German people are about to fall prey to hunger and its terrible consequences'. Young people without any chance of finding a job became increasingly resentful. As *Freies Wort*, a Social Democrat publication, observed: 'There they stand at the street corner: hands in their pockets, hand-rolled cigarettes in their mouths—dissatisfied with themselves and the world: young people, with faces like old people; with faces lacking any trace of energy and vitality; faces full of abysmal, intransigent and hence dangerous hatred against this social order, against their whole environment.'[15]

Fig. 7.1 Index of German industrial production (deseasonalized, 1928 = 100)

On 5 May 1931, preparations for a new austerity package began in earnest, and two days later, Brüning invited his closest advisers to a private dinner to explain his new approach to the reparation issue. The publication of the austerity measures, he suggested, should be combined with a statement indicating that the German people were not willing to make any more sacrifices. Such a manifesto, he believed, would enable the government to signal to the German people a willingness to act in the reparations issue while not actually doing anything that would ruffle the feathers of foreign diplomats and investors.[16]

Brüning knew he was trying to navigate his way between Scylla and Charybdis. 'Domestically, it is necessary to create the impression that the revision of the Young Plan has already been introduced; abroad the impression must prevail that we are doing everything we can to fulfil the Young Plan. The issue has to be kept up in the air until early 1932. Until that point Germany should not allow any negotiations to become critical.' Brüning also explained it would be best to announce the austerity measures just before his visit to the British Prime Minister, Ramsay MacDonald, in early June in order to demonstrate to the world as clearly as possible how desperate Germany's situation had become. To convince his advisers that it was crucial to become more aggressive on the reparations front, Brüning echoed recent conversations with friends of the non-socialist labour movement. Alarmingly, even the non-socialist unions were demanding a revision of the Young Plan and struggling to cope with the spread of Communist ideas within their ranks.[17]

On Monday morning, 11 May 1931, the cabinet approved Brüning's communication strategy and decided to publish the austerity programme in early June just before the trip to England. The train towards a revisionist policy was gathering speed. But a news flash later that day forced every European policymaker to reconsider his options. At 9:30 in the evening, the Austrian Chancellor Otto Ender informed the public that the Österreichische Credit-Anstalt für Handel und Gewerbe (the Austrian Credit Institute for Trade and Business) was insolvent. The Credit-Anstalt, founded in 1855 by Anselm Salomon Freiherr von Rothschild, had quickly become the leading commercial bank of the Austro-Hungarian Empire. In 1931, it was by far the largest financial institution in the country, accounting for 53 per cent of total assets held by all Austrian joint stock banks and doing business with more than 60 per cent of all Austrian limited companies. The write-downs amounted to 140 million Schilling that could barely be covered by the bank's equity capital (125 million Schilling) and open reserves (40 million Schilling). A collapse of this super-bank would have brought down the whole Austrian financial system. Therefore, to calm the public, Ender presented a reconstruction plan. Fresh capital was provided by the government and to a lesser extent by the Austrian National Bank and the Rothschild family.[18]

The Credit-Anstalt crisis raised a number of worrying questions. What would happen if the reconstruction plan did not work? Would the European powers step in to support the bank, or would the crisis spread to Germany and eventually bring down the whole financial edifice of Europe? And what were the political implications of the crisis? Was an Austro-German customs union still a priority for Vienna? How would Berlin react?

There were also doubts over whether Chancellor Otto Ender and Vice-Chancellor Johann Schober were the right people to lead the crisis management. Ender, a member of the conservative Christian Social Party and a long-time governor of the mountainous state of Vorarlberg, had been known for his anti-capitalist sympathies and his anti-Semitic rhetoric. Now he had to rescue the heart of Austrian capitalism whose major shareholder was the Rothschild family. Schober, formerly head of the Vienna police, had concocted the controversial Austro-German customs union plan with German Foreign Minister Curtius. In this function, he had also pressured the Credit-Anstalt in late 1929 to absorb the collapsing Bodencreditanstalt which was one of the main causes for the Credit-Anstalt crisis. Now he was forced to sort out a banking crisis that he had precipitated.

There were good reasons to expect the worst. One of the pessimistic voices was Harry Siepmann, a well-informed senior official at the Bank of England. On the day that the failure of the Credit-Anstalt became known, he called a friend at the Treasury, telling him succinctly: 'This, I think, is it.' Siepmann expected that the crisis would spread to Germany and ultimately to the UK and that 'it may well bring down the whole house of cards in which we have been living'. With respect to events in Austria, Siepmann and other pessimists would prove right. The Credit-Anstalt crisis was not contained, but fully escalated in the weeks after the Ender cabinet announced its reconstruction plan.[19]

From 12 to 16 May, Austrian depositors withdrew more than 300 million Schilling ($42 million) from the bank—more than twice as much as the write-downs (140 million Schilling). By the end of May, it had lost 30 per cent of its deposits. The Credit-Anstalt was forced to turn to the Austrian central bank for the cash required for the exchange of bills. As a result, the volume of notes in circulation exploded, pushing down the official cover ratio from 83 to 68 per cent. That was still comfortably above the threshold of 40 per cent, but the speed of the decline led foreign depositors to withdraw their funds and domestic depositors to change their Schilling into foreign currencies. The Austrian central bank came under enormous pressure.[20]

To pre-finance its reconstruction plan, the Ender cabinet turned to the BIS in Basle. At the end of May, the BIS provided $14 million (100 million Schilling) to the Austrian central bank and demanded in return a state guarantee to reassure the creditors. The parliament duly and unanimously approved the conditions imposed by the BIS. Yet, both the BIS loan and the credit guarantee failed to stop withdrawals and capital flight. Another loan was needed, but disagreement among the BIS central banks blocked the process. France demanded an end to the customs union project before committing more money, but Vice-Chancellor Schober refused to budge, as he had heavily invested in the project. By early June, the Credit-Anstalt crisis threatened to spiral out of control.[21]

Yet, Siepmann and other pessimists proved wrong in that the Austrian crisis did not spill over to Germany. Only on 12 May, the day after the Ender cabinet informed the public, were there signs of contagion. The Darmstädter und Nationalbank (Danat Bank), one of the largest German commercial banks, was believed to have close ties to the Credit-Anstalt which sent its shares down by 5 per cent. But as investors learnt that the volume of German capital invested in Austria was rather small, Danat shares soon recovered. Similarly, German senior officials were convinced that the rest of the German banking sector would not be affected much by the events in Vienna.[22]

The price of the Young Plan bond, a sort of inverse fever curve of the late Weimar Republic, declined in the second half of May, as the Credit-Anstalt crisis escalated. But the Young Plan bond had started its downward trajectory in late April, and the reason behind it was entirely domestic. Investors were alarmed by the rumour that the Brüning cabinet was secretly preparing another austerity programme to avoid a fiscal crisis. Eventually, on Saturday morning, 9 May, the *Vossische Zeitung* confirmed that 'for weeks a desperate struggle has been taking place in the Finance Ministry'. Once more, the liquidity and solvency of the Reich were in doubt.[23]

Investors were also worried about Brüning's weakening position on the domestic front. On 17 May, the Nazis won a sensational victory in the federal state elections of Oldenburg. The party gained 37 per cent of the votes, a stunning advance on its 7.5 per cent in 1928. Oldenburg was a rather small town of about 60,000 inhabitants, but its elections were interpreted as highly symbolic. Goebbels was happy: 'The Oldenburg result has come like a bombshell. We are the masters of the day again.' On the next day, Eduard Dingeldey, parliamentary leader of the German People's Party (DVP) that was part of the cabinet, demanded that the Chancellor show publicly that he was moving towards a renegotiation of reparations with the creditors. A few days later, the non-Communist labour unions united to plead for a revision of the Young Plan. And in the final week of May, the British Labour newspaper *The Daily Herald* claimed that Germany desperately needed another RM 2 billion to avoid a funding crisis. The government rejected the rumour, but failed to calm investors. Now, not only the Young Plan bond weakened, but the Reichsbank also began to lose foreign exchange reserves.[24]

Brüning's trustworthiness in foreign affairs was increasingly questioned. On 19 May, when the pocket battleship A, baptized 'Deutschland', was launched in Kiel, the Chancellor gave a chauvinist speech in front of 56 000 people and President Hindenburg, who was attending the ceremony. In late May, Steel Helmet, the right-wing paramilitary organization, celebrated the 12th Day of the Front-Line Soldiers in Breslau. The French and the Polish were both disgusted and frightened by this gathering, but Brüning would not comment. The Parisian newspaper *Le Temps* attacked the Chancellor: 'What are the leaders responsible for the Reich doing to respond usefully to this behaviour and to justify the trust that we would like to place in a republican and democratic Germany whose peaceful intentions they repeatedly affirm? . . . Instead of calming German public opinion and cautioning against the many dangers of pan-Germanic agitation, the Reich government continues to encourage its people to embrace the most dangerous illusions.' Ten days later, the Polish government sent a diplomatic note to Berlin in which it complained about 'the disturbing moment' created by the gathering of Steel Helmet so near the border.[25]

As the crafting of the austerity package was reaching a conclusion, Brüning needed to decide what he would write in the manifesto. On 30 May, he gathered the cabinet to discuss it. Despite being under pressure to make a bold move, he stuck to his plan: speaking differently to domestic and foreign audiences without taking a concrete step. He thought he could create a sort of illusion. This approach fitted well to the foreboding atmosphere in which the meeting was held. An unusually heavy thunderstorm raged through Berlin, the noise from which made it hard to understand what was said.[26]

Once again the meeting ended inconclusively. Brüning, ever the procrastinator, refused to commit himself to a particular wording. Meanwhile, the austerity package was finalized and approved by President Hindenburg on Wednesday evening, 3 June, only a few hours before Brüning and Curtius left for Chequers. It was a bitter pill to swallow. The main elements were a general spending cut of RM 100 million, a reduction of pensions and insurance benefits, an increase of the sugar tax and oil import duties, the introduction of a crisis tax, and a staggered reduction of civil service wages of between 4 and 6 per cent, including those of the President, the Chancellor, and his ministers. Altogether, wages of top officials had been cut by 30 per cent since the beginning of the crisis.[27]

After receiving Hindenburg's approval, the cabinet discussed Brüning and Curtius's trip to England (Illustration 12). The Chancellor had low expectations: 'The press is making a fuss about the trip. We should apply the brakes a little bit. The British government would like to talk about rearmament issues, whereas

Illustration 12. Chancellor Heinrich Brüning (left), British ambassador Sir Horace Rumbold (centre), and Foreign Minister Julius Curtius (right) at Lehrter train station in Berlin before departing to Chequers.

we have to bring up the reparations question. Surely there will be no agreements at Chequers.' As for the manifesto, the cabinet decided to cable a draft to Brüning while he was on the steamer to England. Shortly before midnight the German delegation boarded the train. Brüning and Curtius were accompanied by only three officials: Erwin Planck of the Chancellery, Leopold Baron von Plessen of the Foreign Ministry, and Paul Schmidt, a Foreign Ministry interpreter. No Finance Ministry technical experts were in the delegation.[28]

The train brought them to Cuxhaven near Hamburg from where they embarked the next morning. What Brüning witnessed on this trip reinforced his impression that he could only stabilize the domestic front by being more aggressive on the question of reparations. Schmidt, the interpreter, wrote in his memoir: 'In order to prevent assassinations and other incidents, the police cordoned off the whole shipyard. We ourselves were "protected" on our short way to the ship by police ranks. But the police had not accounted for the dock workers. When recognizing Brüning, they dropped their ropes or whatever they held in their hands and moved towards us, raising their fists and shouting "Down with the hunger dictator!" It was a critical moment that kept repeating itself on our way to the ship, although the police stepped in.' Brüning was not entirely unhappy about the incident. He knew that news of the unrest would be covered by the international press. It would show the world how dangerous Germany's political situation had become.[29]

The German delegation arrived on Friday morning, 5 June, on the south coast of England. They were taken from their ship to the destroyer HMS *Winchester*, which brought them to Southampton where they were welcomed by the mayor. Then they travelled to London in a special train and arrived at Waterloo Station early in the afternoon. They were greeted by Prime Minister Ramsay MacDonald (Illustration 13), Foreign Secretary Henderson, and 'a large crowd, including many members of the German colony in London', as *The Times* reported. A few hours later, Brüning and Curtius talked to the British and foreign press at the Carlton Hotel, where they would pass their first night on British soil. The Chancellor urged the British public to recognize how dangerous the situation was. 'The present German Government will do all it can to maintain a sound financial policy, but that means imposing an exceptionally great burden on all classes of the population. Political stresses in Germany are very urgent. Radicalism is growing, and we know very well that a solution to all these problems is

Illustration 13. British Prime Minister Ramsay MacDonald.

not possible if we are to rely upon ourselves alone. Such problems are common to all countries. The German Cabinet is convinced that it is only possible to solve them if all the nations of the world genuinely cooperate.'[30]

In the evening, Brüning and Curtius were guests at a banquet given by the Foreign Office. Everybody who was anybody was there: the members of the British cabinet, the High Commissioners of the Dominions residing in London, the Speakers of the House of Commons and the House of Lords, the Archbishop of Canterbury, the leading opposition figures, among them Lloyd George, Stanley Baldwin, and Austin Chamberlain, the generals, the Governor of the Bank of England, the Mayor of London, the presidents of learned societies, and senior officials. Brüning recalled a 'frosty atmosphere'. The after-dinner reception was less formal. Brüning seized the opportunity for individual conversations, especially with Lloyd George, the former Prime Minister.[31]

Later that night, Brüning finally received the text of the manifesto by telegram. It should have arrived during the voyage to Britain, but the cabinet in Berlin had been completely overwhelmed by the task. At the final meeting, the Vice-Chancellor, Finance Minister Dietrich, who was in charge of drafting, got into a heated argument with two other ministers about questions of style. 'Clash of the petit bourgeois about who writes the better German', Schäffer noted in his diary. Dietrich, infuriated by the criticism, eventually left the Chancellery, and his aides had to bring a revised version to his apartment. Whatever the reasons for the delay, Brüning was not happy. The next morning, he told a senior official at the German Foreign Ministry that the wording of the manifesto was too aggressive to be well received by London. One hour later, the German cabinet met to tone it down, as requested by the Chancellor.[32]

After lunch, the German delegation was chauffeured to Chequers, the scenic country retreat of the British Prime Minister, located about 40 miles north-west of London. The cars were followed by journalists and photographers. On arrival, tea was served. Brüning tried to open a serious conversation, but MacDonald and Henderson were reluctant to talk politics. To ease the situation, they all went for a walk and then sat together in the library. Now, a more serious exchange could start. In the first round, there was no rapprochement. Brüning tried to explain the economic and political constraints Germany was confronted with, but his arguments were not well received, especially by Henderson. After two hours, they went for another walk in the park. When they stood by the hedges, Ramsay MacDonald suddenly asked Brüning what he thought about the pessimistic views of Montagu Norman, the Governor of the Bank of England. For Brüning, this was the moment to talk about the world economy and Germany's difficult situation. Bruning felt that MacDonald seemed to be impressed. Having spent nearly three years in London and Manchester while writing his dissertation about 'the relationship of English private railways to the state in times of crisis', Brüning felt at ease speaking English and was able to reach out to MacDonald on an emotional level.[33]

During dinner MacDonald and Brüning did not pursue the matter any further, but discussed religious questions. Surprisingly, the Calvinist Prime Minister and the Catholic Chancellor agreed in many respects. Meanwhile the evening editions of German newspapers published the measures of the second emergency decree and the manifesto that contained the following paragraph:

> We have made every effort to meet our obligations arising from the last war. We have also made extensive use of foreign assistance towards this end. That is no longer possible. By calling on all the energies and reserves of all sections of the population, the German Government has earned the right—and makes it a duty towards its own people—to pronounce to the world: the limit of the privations which we can impose on our people has been reached. The premises on which the Young Plan was based have proved to be erroneous in the light of subsequent events. The Young Plan has failed to give the German people the relief which, according to the intentions of all concerned, it was meant to give and of which it at first held out promise. The Government realizes that the extremely precarious economic and financial situation of the Reich requires that it be relieved of the unbearable reparation obligations. This is also a prerequisite for the economic recovery of the whole world.[34]

The next morning MacDonald did not yet know about the manifesto. But he was agitated by an earthquake that had occurred during the night in eastern and central parts of England—the first for centuries in this area. After breakfast, the formal talks began in the library on the first floor. Sitting at the table were MacDonald, Henderson, the President of the Board of Trade, Brüning, Curtius, and interpreter Schmidt. The group was joined by Sir Robert Vansittart of the Foreign Office and Sir Frederic Leith-Ross of the Treasury, who had motored down from London early in the morning. The atmosphere was relaxed. Shortly after opening the discussion, MacDonald asked the German interpreter, Schmidt, to get a document but Schmidt could not find the door because it was disguised as a bookshelf. The Prime Minister laughed loudly.[35]

Brüning seized the opportunity to repeat what he had explained to MacDonald on the previous day: 'The German Government could not go further without grave danger of social unrest.' The British side acknowledged the economic and political difficulties Brüning was facing, but the conversation was going nowhere. Leith-Ross tried to moderate, but there was no common ground. Brüning felt that the British Foreign Office and the Treasury aligned themselves with the French position and were against any compromise.[36]

At this point, Montagu Norman, the Governor of the Bank of England, entered the scene. After being briefed by the Prime Minister, Norman gave the conversation a completely new turn. He considered the Austrian crisis the most critical point. 'Unless everybody could be got to co-operate in the work of reconstruction, there will be a catastrophe.' To the Germans, Norman said: 'I do not wish to belittle the difficulties of the German Government, but it is a less urgent problem. Germany has already gone through two or three financial crises which would have been fatal to any other country; she has shown a wonderful power of recuperation, and she may well get through again.'[37]

With respect to the Credit-Anstalt crisis, Montagu Norman was right. The situation had in fact become highly dangerous. The French were still blocking a second BIS loan, as Austria was not willing to give up the customs union project with Germany, and Vice-Chancellor Schober still refused to compromise. It would take another week until the Austrian crisis was contained. Norman played a crucial role. The Bank of England stepped in with an emergency short-term credit, and a consortium of foreign creditors accepted a standstill agreement.[38]

With respect to the German situation, however, Norman completely underestimated the danger, and MacDonald and the other British officials shared his view. Though sympathetic to the German situation, they were not willing to offer any help. The conversation was adjourned, but then took another, unexpected course. During the adjournment, Sir Robert Vansittart brought in telegrams from the British ambassador in Washington. As soon as the two parties met again to continue their conversation, MacDonald told Brüning: 'I have just received three important telegrams from Washington showing that the manifesto issued in Berlin yesterday, as reported by American newspapers, has made a very unfavourable impression in the United States, and is regarded as likely to affect Germany's credit in America seriously.'[39]

It was an awkward situation. More than twelve hours after the publication of the manifesto, the British Prime Minister, sitting together with Brüning and Curtius, was unaware of it. Only after the British ambassador in the United States had called London did MacDonald catch up with the course of events. It was not that the British Sunday papers had failed to report the news from Germany.

But as it did not make headlines, nobody seemed to notice. For example, the *Sunday Times* reported about both the emergency decree and the manifesto, but the article was short and buried on page 15. It was also embarrassing for the German side. The plan was to signal to the domestic audience that the government was determined to seek a revision of the reparations agreement, while not upsetting foreign governments, diplomats, and investors. Obviously, the execution of the plan had failed spectacularly and now started to backfire.[40]

MacDonald proposed to read the telegrams aloud to the Germans. Brüning then responded somewhat surprised: 'I cannot understand why Washington should be so upset. The manifesto contains no reference to a moratorium; it merely repeats the declaration that both I and Dr. Curtius have already made several times in the Reichstag.' MacDonald replied: 'A published statement often makes a more serious impression than statements made in the course of a parliamentary speech.' And Montagu Norman added: 'The last passage, viz., "that the economic and financial situation of the Reich inevitably compels the relief of Germany from intolerable reparation obligations", is pretty emphatic. I have not seen this text before, and I can well understand the repercussions in America. It seems to me that this declaration entirely alters the situation. I hope very much that the German Government does not have any more surprises like this to spring during the next few weeks.' Curtius tried to reassure him: 'There are no more manifestos in preparation.'

MacDonald wrapped up the meeting: 'I do not think we can carry matters further. It will be necessary to issue a communiqué to the press and we will have to give our French friends and the Italians an account of the discussion which has taken place.' Some

English and German officials soon came up with a draft. The communiqué contained the following paragraph: 'Special stress was laid by the German Ministers on the difficulties of the existing position in Germany and the need for alleviation.' Negotiations lasted until 6 p.m., then both parties separated. Brüning recalled: 'The farewell was gracious, but depressed.'[41]

The rest of the trip lifted the spirits. Later that day, Brüning was invited by Archibald Church, a Labour MP who had played an important role in getting MacDonald to invite Brüning to Chequers. The next day, he met Walter Layton, the editor of *The Economist*, and had an audience with King George V, who spoke uninterrupted for twenty minutes, reviewing a series of budget and debt data. He also had a long conversation with Chancellor Snowden who shared many of Brüning's concerns. In the afternoon, he gave a speech at the Royal Institute of International Affairs (Chatham House). 'When I entered', Brüning wrote in his memoirs, 'I felt that the spell was broken. I was welcomed with great applause.' The visit concluded with a widely attended reception at the German embassy.[42]

Nevertheless, when they left London on Tuesday morning, 9 June, Brüning and Curtius knew they had achieved very little. They were further disillusioned when they met American ambassador Sackett and his wife coming back from the United States on the German ship *Europa*. Once more, Sackett did not bring encouraging news. 'America cannot help directly', he told the Germans. What was more, the Second Emergency Decree had unleashed a 'hurricane' in the country, as Brüning's Chief of Staff Pünder put it. The manifesto was well received in Germany, but did not help calming the opposition against the next round of austerity. Moreover, it triggered a run on the German currency, as investors feared that Germany would become insolvent.[43]

When the German delegation, together with the American ambassador and his wife, disembarked in Bremerhaven, they were confronted with crowds even angrier than those that had confronted them when they had left Germany a couple of days earlier. This time, not only Communist dock workers but also Nazis demonstrated. Germany once more dominated the international news cycle. In its 15 June edition of *Time* magazine, Brüning's austere face was on the cover: 'New Germany's Iron Chancellor.'[44]

8

HELP FROM WASHINGTON

The run on the German currency rapidly gained momentum. Foreign investors withdrew their funds from German banks in rising numbers which, in turn, rushed to the Reichsbank to obtain the necessary foreign exchange to pay to their fleeing depositors. In the first week of June, the Reichsbank's gold and foreign exchange reserves declined by RM 163 million or 6 per cent. And on Wednesday, 10 June, when Brüning returned to Berlin, the Reichsbank lost nearly RM 70 million more. The cover ratio—the share of gold and foreign reserves relative to banknotes in circulation—was rapidly approaching the legal minimum of 40 per cent. Germany's adherence to the gold standard was increasingly called into question.[1]

Yet, the run on the German currency was not the only problem Brüning had to cope with after his trip to England. In early June, disturbing news regarding the stability of the second largest commercial bank, the Darmstädter und Nationalbank (Danat Bank), had emerged in the press. First, the Communist tabloid *Welt am Abend* spread the rumour that Danat was about to fail. Then, the mainstream press published articles about a huge write-down by the textile business Nordwolle, headquartered in Bremen. Nordwolle was one of Danat's most important industrial clients. The façade of the German banking system began to crack.[2]

To be sure, there was no banking crisis yet. The three other large banks headquartered in Berlin with extended branch networks—Deutsche Bank, Dresdner Bank, and Commerzbank— were believed to be solid. And two other large banks without branch networks, the Berliner Handelsgesellschaft and the Reichskreditgesellschaft (owned by the Reich), were also coping well. Yet Danat had the same business model as Deutsche, Dresdner, and Commerzbank. They all relied to a large extent on foreign short-term deposits which made them highly vulnerable to a currency crisis. Danat's problems with Nordwolle were serious, but only became dangerous because at the same time the bank was suffering from the withdrawal of foreign deposits. Losses both on the liability and the asset side prepared the ground for a banking crisis.[3]

Danat was the first bank to be in trouble because of its aggressive catch-up strategy in the 1920s. Formed out of the Darmstädter Bank für Handel und Gewerbe and the Nationalbank in 1922 to become the fourth largest bank, it tried to establish itself as the country's leading financial institution. The driving force was the energetic managing director Jakob Goldschmidt, who also owned a considerable stake in Danat shares. The son of a merchant of modest means near Hannover, Goldschmidt made his career as an independent trader on the Berlin stock exchange. In 1918, at the age of 36, he became a member of the executive board of the Nationalbank together with Hjalmar Schacht who left Danat one year after the merger to become head of the Reichsbank.[4]

It was unusual for a former stock market trader to rise to the top of a large universal bank, and it made a real difference. Under his leadership, Danat focused on investment banking, buying shares of large industrial firms and facilitating mergers and acquisitions.

For example, Goldschmidt was instrumental in forming the Vereinigte Stahlwerke and underwriting the expansion of Nordwolle. His next plan, to create a conglomerate in the automobile industry after the model of General Motors, ultimately failed, but showed his ambition to become the impresario of Germany's corporate world. By 1931, Goldschmidt sat on the board of no fewer than 123 German corporations. Danat also specialized in financing local authorities, which made Goldschmidt widely known in political circles. And it always paid considerably higher dividends than its competitors. To fuel Danat's rapid expansion, Goldschmidt resorted to debt financing on a large scale, of which a considerable part was foreign and short-term. The bank's capital ratio—that is, the proportion of a bank's own resources to its total assets—in 1929 was only 4.8 per cent, insufficient to absorb a major economic shock. The capital ratios of Deutsche, Commerzbank, and Dresdner were 8.3 per cent, 6.1 per cent, and 5.7 per cent respectively.[5]

Goldschmidt was not concerned about his dependence on foreign short-term credit or his close ties with industrial clients. On the contrary, in public speeches he advocated financial globalization as the right way to push Germany forward. Accordingly he was flabbergasted when he was informed in mid-May about Nordwolle's huge losses and that not only the Danat, but also Dresdner was strongly affected, even though to a lesser extent. The news was brought to him by Max Doerner, a Danat manager, who had hired a detective to find out the true state of Nordwolle. Goldschmidt was shattered, shouting: 'Nordwolle is finished, the Danat Bank is finished, the Dresdner Bank is finished. I am finished.' The next day, when he spoke to G. Carl Lahusen, the General Director of Nordwolle, Goldschmidt threw a chair at Lahusen's head out of anger and despair.[6]

Given that Danat was an extreme case, but not an exception, investors began to realize that not only Germany's fiscal position but also the stability of its banking system was threatened. The only bright spot was that domestic savers were not panicking yet. The volume of banknotes held by the public did not increase in late May and early June.[7] But how long would German savers remain patient?

On top of the mounting financial and monetary problems, Brüning had to deal with an escalating political crisis. 'The outcry about the emergency decree has grown to a hurricane,' as State Secretary Pünder observed. The Communists, the Nazis, and Hugenberg's National People's Party agreed on a joint attack against the new austerity measures, with the ultimate aim of removing the Brüning cabinet. Their plan was to force the Reichstag to reconvene. That would make a partial German government default quite probable, the extremist parties reckoned. And the resulting financial chaos would force Hindenburg to sack Brüning.

There was a real chance that the radical parties would succeed in gaining a majority of the Council of Elders of the Reichstag, a body of twenty-three deputies in which all parties were represented according to their proportional strength. The Council of Elders had the power to decide whether the Reichstag should reconvene. On Thursday, 11 June 1931, the deputies of the German People's Party (DVP) endorsed their plan to reconvene the Reichstag, although, as part of the ruling coalition, they were supposed to go along with the austerity programme. Before the crucial DVP meeting took place, Brüning made it clear to his ministers that he would resign if the Reichstag reconvened. And at the meeting itself Foreign Minister Curtius warned his fellow party members not to join the extremist parties' plot, but it was to no avail. Shortly before midnight the vote took place, with fifteen deputies voting for and thirteen deputies against reconvening the Reichstag. A partial default of the Reich became a real possibility.[8]

Meanwhile, the Communist Party heightened the pressure by organizing so-called 'hunger marches' in Berlin, Hamburg, and other major cities. Clashes between Communist streetfighters and the police were particularly violent in the evening of Thursday, 11 June, with the most extreme one occurring in Kassel. As the *Vossische Zeitung* reported, Communist troops attacked the police with firearms around 11:30 p.m., which led the police to shoot back. Although the officers mostly shot in the air, several people were wounded, and a 90-year-old shoemaker, who was hit by a ricocheted bullet, was found dead in his apartment. The riots continued until after midnight. The police arrested forty-five Communists, including one who was suspected of having shot dead a police constable the night before. The 'hunger marches' continued for another three days.[9]

One day later, on Friday, 12 June, the political crisis in Berlin reached a new stage. The Social Democratic deputies threatened to endorse the motion to reconvene the Reichstag if Brüning did not promise a concession regarding youth unemployment benefits. On the same day, the Chancellor went to see President Hindenburg at his family estate in Neudeck in Prussia to brief him on the England talks and the current situation in Berlin. Hindenburg backed the Chancellor, telling him to stick to his plan. He also gave him the authority to organize the Reichswehr in case of an emergency. Obviously, Brüning was not excluding the possibility of civil unrest on a large scale.[10]

Frightened by the escalating political crisis, investors accelerated their capital withdrawals. On Friday, 12 June, when the Social

Democrats attacked Brüning, the calls on central bank reserves reached a new daily record: no less than RM 200 million were withdrawn. On the following day, after the markets closed, the Reichsbank board convened an extraordinary meeting at 5 p.m. and decided to raise the official interest rate from 5 to 7 per cent to stem the tide. A joyful Goebbels wrote in his diary: 'Brüning battles for his existence. If he falls, we are next. The catastrophe is just outside the door.'[11]

Brüning would not give up, however. On Monday, 15 June, he made another attempt to muster a majority in the Council of Elders of the Reichstag. He convened a meeting of all party leaders of the ruling coalition, hoping to be able to soften them up until they would give in. He excluded the parliamentary leaders of the Social Democratic Party in the first round, preferring to bank on those party members who held high government positions: President of the Reichstag Paul Löbe, Prussian Minister President Otto Braun, and Prussian Interior Minister Carl Severing. Both Braun and Severing depended on the support of Brüning's Centre Party. If they refused to endorse the Chancellor, they risked losing their majority in the Prussian parliament.[12]

Brüning used all his rhetorical skills to intimidate them. Luther endorsed him by painting a dramatic picture of the Reichsbank's gold and foreign reserve positions. After nearly two hours, all party leaders except Löbe, Braun, and Severing left the room. Now the parliamentary leaders of the Social Democrats were allowed to join the discussion. Again, Brüning and Luther portrayed the future in the darkest colours, if the Reichstag reconvened. Later, Brüning, Luther, and some ministers met with leaders of parties that were not represented in the cabinet. The conversations lasted until midnight.[13]

The strategy had some success, but the fight was not over yet. The next morning, 16 June, Brüning received a secret message from Otto Braun that the Social Democrats were against reconvening the Reichstag, but continued to insist on calling the Budget Committee. This was still not acceptable to the Chancellor. He needed an unequivocal endorsement of his austerity programme and told his cabinet that he would submit his resignation to President Hindenburg if the Social Democrats prevailed. All ministers fell into line. At noon, the Council of Elders of the Reichstag met to decide whether the Reichstag should reconvene. Pünder transmitted the resolution of the cabinet to resign if the wish of the Chancellor was ignored. The Council of Elders decided not to reconvene the Reichstag, but as the Social Democrats still insisted on reconvening the Budget Committee, a final decision could not be reached. A new round of negotiations started. At 6 p.m. the Council of Elders met again and eventually decided to go along with the wishes of the Chancellor. The radical parties were isolated, because the People's Party and the Social Democrats had come together to endorse the Chancellor.[14]

Brüning's victory averted a full-blown crisis for the time being. State Secretary Pünder felt great relief after expecting the worst: 'A day of enormous importance is now drawing to a close. Soon it is midnight. But I still have to put a few impressions on paper. *We won!* Strong pressure has been taken from us. Out there, life was taking its course, and only the fewest people knew or sensed that perhaps a civil war was looming. In fourteen days we would not have been able to pay the salaries, old-age pensions, war pensions etc. without today's result. But we won!'[15]

The resolution of the political crisis only slowed down the run on the German currency temporarily. On Friday, 19 June 1931, three days after Brüning's victory, the Reichsbank lost gold and foreign exchange reserves amounting to nearly RM 70 million. The cover ratio was now barely above the legal minimum of 40 per cent. To protect its reserves, the Reichsbank decided to restrict the payment of banknotes in exchange for bills offered by private banks. This measure, however, did nothing to alleviate the crisis. It merely put more pressure on the banks which needed access to the foreign exchange reserves of the Reichsbank to compensate for the decline of their foreign short-term deposits.[16]

On Wednesday, 17 June, the textile concern Nordwolle officially confirmed its financial problems: RM 24 million of direct losses and RM 30 million of losses of its subsidiaries. The accumulated debt amounted to RM 136 million, while the capital stock accounted for only RM 75 million. Nordwolle also disclosed that its debts vis-à-vis Danat amounted to RM 20 million. Danat shares immediately came under pressure. Other banks began to falter under the burden of the slump and the currency crisis, notably the Landesbank of the Rheinprovinz. In the boom of the 1920s this bank had recklessly transformed short-term deposits into long-term loans to West German cities and municipalities that were now cash-strapped as a result of the economic crisis. When its first losses appeared, the executive board hid the true figures from the supervisory authorities in the Prussian Ministry of the Interior. But eventually, a senior official discovered the losses and reported them to Berlin. The cabinet was informed on Thursday, 18 June.[17]

The government was caught on the back foot because it had received little information about the banks' problems on a regular basis. For example, the Reichsbank did not hear about Nordwolle until 12 June, and strangely enough, it did not get the information from a German source, but from the Bank of England. A sense of despair began to spread. Fritz Mannheimer, the flamboyant director of the Amsterdam branch of the German investment bank Mendelssohn & Co., came to see Hans Schäffer on Friday evening, 19 June. 'Mannheimer comes before his departure, very agitated', Schäffer wrote in his diary. 'He sees the things here as the prelude to the collapse that will engulf everybody in the abyss.' *The Economist* mused that it was doubtful 'whether, at any period since the world depression developed in 1930, those responsible for guiding financial and economic affairs have had a more anxious time than during the last ten days'.[18]

But then, out of the blue, the series of bad news was interrupted by a hopeful message from Washington. On Saturday morning, 20 June, the German newspapers reported that US President Herbert Hoover was 'taking the initiative'. On the evening before, Hoover had informed the American press of his conversations with congressional leaders about ways to foster economic recovery in the United States and Europe and to support Germany. It was not clear, however, how to interpret the message from Washington, as Hoover had remained vague: 'These conversations have been particularly directed to strengthening the situation in Germany. No definite plans or conclusions have yet been arrived at but the response which I have met from the leaders of both parties is most gratifying. Any statement of any plan or method is wholly speculative and is not warranted by the facts.'[19]

Thus, German officials were still in the dark on Saturday morning, and most of them were so dejected by the ongoing economic crisis that they dared not raise their hopes. When State Secretary Schäffer was told by an American journalist stationed in Berlin that Hoover was thinking about a partial cancellation of all war-related debts, he declined to respond. And Reichsbank President

Luther, exhausted by the ongoing currency crisis, remained pessimistic. He called Schäffer to tell him that the Reichsbank continued to lose tens of millions in foreign exchange reserves. Even ordinary people were now seeking the stability of foreign money. Schäffer urged Luther to call Governor Montagu Norman in London to obtain credit from the Bank of England and other central banks. Luther was reluctant, but eventually called Norman. The conversation did not go well.[20]

At 4:30 p.m., Brüning's economic team was scheduled to discuss the reparations issue.[21] As it was still not clear what Hoover had in mind, everybody expected that the cabinet would opt for a moratorium on reparation payments. But then another surprising message came in ten minutes before the meeting: US ambassador Sackett called the Chancellery, revealing that he had just received an urgent telephone call from Washington, advising him that Hoover planned to announce a one-year moratorium of all war-related debts. Sackett said he would come to the Chancellery as soon as he had received the cable confirming the message, Brüning was completely taken aback, as the idea of a moratorium was not even on the table.[22]

At 5:15 p.m. Sackett arrived at the Chancellery. He outlined Hoover's plan to call for a one year moratorium of all war-related debts and explained that the US President needed a request from the German government to rally domestic support for it. To sell it to the American people, Sackett added, Hoover needed a statement by President Hindenburg describing Germany's grave economic plight, and hinting at the importance of temporary debt relief. Sackett needed a quick response, as Hoover wanted to be sure that the Germans endorsed his plan. But President Hindenburg was still on his estates in Neudeck. A first draft was prepared, but it was an enormously difficult process, as several German ministers and senior officials wanted to have a say. At 8:30 p.m. the general approval was transmitted from Neudeck, and an hour later, Brüning and Sackett met again to finalize the draft. It took more than four hours to write the final version. At 2 a.m. Berlin time and 8 p.m. Washington time, Hindenburg's letter was encoded in its English text and sent to the White House.[23]

As it turned out, Hindenburg's telegram came too late. Hoover's plan had been leaked, forcing the White House to hold a press conference and issue a statement before the official request from Germany had reached Washington. In any event, the ball had started rolling. Hoover's statement started with the sentence: 'The American Government proposes the postponement for one year of all payments on intergovernmental debts, reparations, and relief debts, both principal and interest, of course, not including obligations of governments held by private parties.'[24]

Why did Hoover (Illustration 14) take this initiative? Back in February 1931, when he had been asked by Ambassador Sackett to help Berlin, he showed no desire to make a bold move. Now, all of a sudden, he was determined to act. Records show that the President had worried about Germany for quite some time, and gradually had come to the realization that doing nothing was likely to be more costly than taking a risk. A German financial collapse would not only freeze private American credit but also destabilize the US economy. In this respect, Hoover's statement was entirely sincere: 'The purpose of this action is to give the forthcoming year to the economic recovery of the world and to help free the recuperative forces already in motion in the United States from retarding influences from abroad.'[25]

The idea of a moratorium was not new. Ever since Hitler won his sensational victory in the elections of September 1930, it had

Illustration 14. US President Herbert Hoover.

been discussed in New York and Washington. American private creditors involved in Germany were pressing particularly hard for a reduction of reparations and all other war-related debts. But most politicians in Washington were convinced that the American people would never accept a debt moratorium. In October 1930, Hoover told Eugene Meyer, the new chairman of the Federal Reserve, that debt reduction was politically impossible. Meyer was not convinced, but until early May 1931 the President stuck to his conviction.[26]

A series of conversations and events then seemed to push Hoover towards thinking the unthinkable. An important contribution came from his conversation on 6 May with Ambassador Sackett, who was vacationing in the USA for a few weeks. 'The situation is gradually developing towards a critical climax', the ambassador told the President. 'I don't feel that there is any immediate danger, but I am convinced that unless the economic tide turns by fall the German situation must collapse.' Hoover asked the ambassador: 'Do you think a suspension of reparations under the Young Plan would do any good?' Sackett replied firmly: 'I think it would help.' Hoover promised to study the situation and discuss it with Sackett at the end of the month. Sackett then went to a dinner with Secretary of State Henry Stimson to repeat his warning. The next day, 7 May, Hoover requested the Commerce Department and the State Department to provide all information on intergovernmental debt, military expenditure, and trade.[27]

A few days later, Hoover talked to Stimson about what Sackett had told him. For the first time, Hoover hinted at the possibility 'that the depression had reached such depths as to make the whole fabric of intergovernmental debt beyond the capacity to pay under depression conditions'. In the following days, Hoover got the news of the escalating Credit-Anstalt crisis which reinforced his sense that something had to be done. 'That confirms Sackett's view of the dangers in that quarter', he noted in his diary.[28]

At the same time, Hoover reached out to the German delegates who attended the meeting of the International Chamber of Commerce in Washington from 4 to 7 May. He got the clear impression that the Germans 'took the gloomiest view'. On 8 May, the Belgian delegates were invited to a dinner at the White House. The situation in Belgium, they stated, was 'not bad', but in Germany it was 'very bad, both socially and economically'.[29]

Yet, at this point, Hoover was not yet ready to consider real action. He was not a person who took a risk lightly as he liked time for reflection. 'I recognized that the president was following his usual psychological reaction to a proposition like this', Stimson later noted in his diary. 'In every important crisis which I have had with him . . . he has always gone through a period in which he sees every possible difficulty and gets terribly discouraged over it.' Thus, when on 2 June Sackett called at the White House before sailing back to Germany, Hoover gave him a non-committal response, explaining that 'we would need to assist in the crisis, and that he could assure the German Government that we would endeavour to be helpful. I told him of my view that the whole reparations and debt complex could well be [temporarily] reviewed in the light of capacity to pay under depression conditions, and that he might advise upon his arrival the reaction from the German Government.'[30]

Hoover drafted a first statement proposing a moratorium and presented it on 5 June in a meeting with Stimson, Secretary of the Treasury, Andrew Mellon, and his Undersecretary Ogden Mills. Stimson liked the idea, while Mellon and Mills entirely disapproved. Hoover concluded that he needed yet more information. He advised Mills to go to New York to talk to bankers and asked Mellon, who was about to leave for his vacation in Europe, to make independent enquiries during this trip. On 10 June, Mellon set sail for London on the Mauretania. Asked by journalists if he was going to discuss the question of reparations, he replied: 'I am sorry if people should think so, but I am not.' He merely wanted to visit his son who was taking his post-graduate degree at Cambridge.[31]

Hoover was finally pushed to take action by the German currency crisis triggered by the manifesto of 6 June and the provocative Brüning cabinet declaration that 'the limit of the privations which we can impose on our people has been reached'. While spending the weekend of 13 and 14 June at 'the Rapidan', his modest wooden house in the forests of Virginia, Hoover received several calls from Stimson and Mills, reporting that the statements made by the German government 'had precipitated runs on Central European banks and that a crisis had developed much more rapidly than had been anticipated'. He was also informed by Secretary of the Treasury Mellon, who was still on board the RMS *Mauretania*, that 'the situation was absolutely critical'. Mellon had completely changed his opinion.[32]

On Monday, 15 June, Stimson sent a message to his ambassador, Charles Dawes, in London, telling him that he should contact Mellon after his arrival in England and encourage him to talk to MacDonald. Mellon arrived in London on Tuesday evening, 16 June, and convinced Dawes to support a moratorium. Mellon then talked to MacDonald and Montagu Norman to get their views on the German situation and immediately transmitted their pessimistic outlook to Washington. From 15 to 17 June, Hoover was on a speaking tour taking in West Virginia, Indiana, Ohio, and Illinois. Because he had recognized that there was no going back, he talked to congressional leaders during his train trip through the Midwest. His idea of a moratorium fell on fertile ground. Hoover also received a series of telegrams from Berlin in which Sackett advocated swift action. Arriving back in Washington on Thursday, 18 June, he continued talks with congressional leaders who, with the odd exception, endorsed his plan. Originally, Hoover wanted to publish the moratorium proposal the following week.[33]

But it proved impossible to keep such a far-reaching plan secret after all the consultations with Congress. On Saturday evening, 20 June, after some journalists had heard of the plan, he held a press conference and made his plan public.

When the statement was released, investors reacted euphorically. On Monday, 22 June, the Dow Jones Industrial Average jumped by more than 10 per cent and continued to rise through to the end of the week by another 6 per cent. The Young Plan bond quoted in Amsterdam and London climbed by more than 10 per cent on the day after the news broke; the Young Plan bond quoted in Paris by 7 per cent. The Young Plan bond was now back at the value it had had before the German manifesto of 6 June. The Reichsbank immediately loosened the credit restrictions it had introduced only recently, giving banks access to its gold and foreign exchange reserves.[34]

In political terms, Hoover's plan was welcomed in Berlin and London. Prime Minister MacDonald gave his full endorsement, and the British press reacted positively. The Times editorialized that President Hoover 'has given a wise lead in the worldwide difficulties raised by the problem of inter-Governmental debts and War Reparations. If it is rapidly followed by the wisely concerted action of others it should check a series of financial collapses that are threatening the economic, social, and political fabric of Europe, the repercussions of which would be felt far beyond its boundaries.'[35]

Likewise, the German mainstream press endorsed the Hoover moratorium. Chancellor Brüning welcomed Hoover's initiative in a public speech: 'All the peoples of the earth are deeply impressed by the historic step taken by the President of the United States on Sunday to check the dreadful crisis which has overtaken almost all nations and to bring aid to those who are about to succumb to it. The German people and the German Government accept President Hoover's proposal with heartfelt gratitude. We see a new hope for Europe and for Germany proceeding from this proposal.'[36]

Only the radical German parties were dismayed. The financial chaos they had hoped for did not occur. Goebbels wrote in his diary: 'The Hoover offer really hurts. It will postpone our victory by about four months. It makes me sick! Middle-class Germans are just so stupid.'[37]

9

ENDGAME

Two days after Hoover announced his plan, the British economist John Maynard Keynes was in Chicago to deliver a series of lectures on unemployment. As the Hoover moratorium was on everyone's lips, Keynes offered his view before treating the announced topic. He considered it 'a fine piece of policy', but 'not the best possible'. The main problem in the short run, he argued, was that the proposal called 'for a substantial sacrifice on the part of France'. Keynes predicted that the French government would 'begin by resisting such a sacrifice'.[1]

Keynes was right. While most governments in Europe welcomed the Hoover moratorium, French officials were reluctant, to say the least, to go along. In his first reaction, Paul Claudel, the French ambassador in Washington, cabled to Paris that the proposal 'bears all the marks of suddenness and exaggeration that are the characteristics of any American action, but there is no doubt that it responds to pressure by bankers'. The French press reacted similarly. The right-wing paper *Le Figaro* sneered that Hoover's plan was 'an improvised diplomatic document of the most disconcerting character'. And like Claudel, *Le Figaro* was convinced that Hoover was a puppet of Wall Street. Eugène Lautier, a liberal deputy close to Parisian business circles, considered the moratorium 'an attack by President Hoover on our national purse'. The pro-government newspaper *Le Temps* was more restrained, but shared Lautier's position. On the Left, the initial reactions were positive. Léon Blum welcomed Hoover's plan because he expected that international financial cooperation would lead to a round of disarmament. Yet, only two days later, Blum showed himself more sceptical, speaking of 'the necessity of avoiding any confusion' and insisting that Germany continue to pay at least a part of its reparations. And *L'Ère nouvelle*, a newspaper close to the Socialist labour movement, wrote: 'Mr Hoover commands France to comply the same way he would command Nicaragua, and the whole world is surprised at us pursing our lips.' Caught by surprise by the course of events, many French politicians suspected they were victims of an Anglo-German conspiracy. On Sunday afternoon, 21 June, Finance Minister Flandin told US ambassador Walter Edge at a reception in Paris: 'This announcement, following so soon after Mr. Mellon's presence in London and after the Chequers meeting raised some suspicions in Parliamentary circles.' He himself did not think that the conspiracy theory was true, Flandin reassured the American ambassador. But he made it clear that some deputies felt that this announcement was the outcome of secret meetings that had excluded France.[2]

Sensing that French resistance would be difficult to overcome, Washington stepped up its campaign for the moratorium. On Monday, 22 June, Secretary of State Stimson contacted Treasury Secretary Mellon in London and asked him to go to Paris as soon as possible. 'We feel that such a visit would just at this time do more than anything else to secure French acceptance, although we of course dislike breaking into your vacation in this way.' The State Department clearly had no sympathy for the French position. 'The French are the most hopeless people in the world,'

Undersecretary Castle wrote in his diary on 23 June, 'they are quibbling about methods while the house burns.'[3]

On Wednesday, 24 June, the French government spelled out why it rejected Hoover's proposal in its present form. Above all, it was adamantly against suspending the so-called unconditional annuities of the Young Plan—that is, the part of reparation payments that according to the agreement was never to be suspended—regardless of the circumstances. If a debt moratorium was introduced, the French government argued, 'there would be great risk of shaking confidence in the value of signatures and contracts, and thus of proceeding contrary to the overall aim' The French government also doubted 'that the mere suspension of payments would furnish an inadequate remedy'. It saw the root of the problem elsewhere: 'The dangers now threatening the German economy and, more generally, the European economy have another origin and are especially due to important restrictions on credit and withdrawals of foreign funds. The solution to the German crisis, therefore, does not appear to lie only in the diminution of the charges on the budget of the Reich, but in an extension of credit.'[4]

To appear constructive, the French government came up with its own plan. It proposed that Germany would pay the unconditional annuity as usual to the Bank for International Settlements (BIS). But the French government would make its own part of the annuity available to private enterprises in Germany and other crisis-stricken countries in Central Europe rather than keep it for its own use. The plan also foresaw that in the year after the moratorium, the Germans would have to pay back this money. In this way, the French argued, the legal core of the Young Plan—the unconditional annuity—was preserved without inflicting economic harm in the short run.[5]

The deeper reason why the cabinet opposed the Hoover moratorium was the expected opposition in parliament, as US ambassador Edge told his superiors in Washington. The German ambassador Leopold von Hoesch came to the same conclusion. On 24 June, he cabled to Berlin: 'The overall impression is one of an extraordinary uproar, resentment, and nervousness. If you don't live in the local atmosphere, you can hardly form an idea of the state of mind into which the French political world was thrown by Hoover's initiative.' He also cited the Vice President of the Chamber of Deputies telling him the day before that 'the French parliament had not been in such an agitated state since the Armistice'.[6]

That observation was no exaggeration. The debate in the Chamber of Deputies was intense, starting on Friday afternoon, 26 June, at 3 p.m. and not ending until 6:30 the next morning. Eventually, the vote of no-confidence was clearly rejected by 386 to 189 votes, but Prime Minister Pierre Laval well understood that he had little room for manoeuvre after being grilled by several speakers. His cabinet survived only because the Socialists, his political opponents, endorsed him, while dozens of deputies of his own coalition refused to stay in line. After the debate, Laval told the German ambassador von Hoesch that he needed a delegation of German ministers to come to Paris as soon as possible, if he was to stay in power and save the Hoover moratorium.[7]

In view of the strong opposition of the French parliament, it was unrealistic to expect that France and the United States would come rapidly to any understanding. A large majority of French deputies were set firmly against suspending the unconditional annuity. The Americans, for their part, rejected the French counter-proposal for two reasons. First, the German government would have to pay a higher sum in the first year after the end of the moratorium than before it. 'Such a proposition contains no element of relief to Germany', they argued. Second, the French government wanted not only Germany, but also other Central European nations such as Poland and Czechoslovakia that were allied to France, to be entitled to use the funds paid to the BIS. The Americans, by contrast, were convinced that Germany needed as much relief as possible.[8]

In addition, the Americans feared that, by delaying the process, the French government was about to kill the psychological effect of the moratorium plan. As early as Sunday, 21 June, Secretary of State Stimson had explained to Ambassador Claudel that 'time was of the essence, the crisis was one of confidence and credit, and therefore the psychological element played a large part in how it would play out'. The central idea in Hoover's proposition, Stimson reminded Claudel, was that 'a wise creditor gives time to his debtor, and the moratorium aimed to provide time to the government debtors of Central Europe for one year so that they could recover their breath and get on their feet'. The admonition clearly failed to have the desired effect.[9]

Could the US President have achieved his goal if he had chosen a different approach? There is no doubt that Hoover's initiative was clumsy. The French government had good reasons to feel duped. It is also doubtful whether a one-year moratorium would have ended the worldwide depression. On the other hand, the advanced stage of the German crisis required swift action. Starting a discussion with Paris would have taken time, leading to press leaks that would have shattered financial markets. More importantly, French resistance to granting another concession to Germany ran deep, regardless of the specific proposals. The experience after the evacuation of the Rhineland had been traumatic. Most French citizens felt that their generosity had been exploited by German leaders. They could not understand why Paris was supposed to help a country that, from the French perspective, took compromise for weakness.[10]

Even Prime Minister Laval and Foreign Minister Briand, two political heavyweights, were powerless in the face of negative public sentiment. When they proposed to proceed in the same way as the Belgian government, namely to accept the Hoover moratorium in principle, while leaving the negotiations of details to a later round, they were endorsed only by three members of the cabinet: Finance Minister Flandin, Colonial Minister Reynaud, and François-Poncet, Undersecretary of the National Economy. The same gap was apparent during the parliamentary debate. Even the argument put forward by Finance Minister Flandin—that the alternative to the Hoover plan would be a unilateral moratorium declared by the Germans—failed to convince the deputies.[11]

Given this strong opposition, the argument that the figures were unfavourable for the French government is secondary. It is true that of the European powers France had to deal with the greatest net loss (Table 9.1). But even a better deal would not have removed French doubts. For the real issue was not financial, but how to maintain security against an increasingly restive neighbour that was stronger in terms of both population and economic capacity. Sooner or later, this would translate into military superiority. At this point, reparations were France's only instrument to delay Germany's domination.

Still, although French politicians had good reasons to be reluctant, they were not entirely free of responsibility. For months, the French embassy in Berlin had been informing the Foreign Ministry

Table 9.1 Financial effects of the Hoover Plan on Germany and its most important creditor countries

	Suspended receipts (£000s)	Suspended payments (£000s)	Net loss (–) or gain (+) (£000s)
United States	53,600	Nil	−53,600
Great Britain[a]	42,500	32,800	−9,700
France	39,700	23,600	−16,100
Italy	9,200	7,400	−1,800
Belgium	5,100	2,700	−2,400
Germany	Nil	77,000	+77,000

[a] The exceptionally large British debit balance is accounted for by the war debts of the Dominions, reconstruction debts and other items excluded from the scope of the Balfour Note.
(*Source*: *The Economist*, 12 November 1932, War Debts Supplement, p. 10.)

of the unfolding collapse in Germany. For example, on 7 May, the financial attaché warned Paris that between mid-June and early August the issue of reparations would be officially called into question. But the French government never seriously developed a plan or initiated a concerted action with Britain and the United States. It always defended the status quo, although many politicians realized that their country was increasingly isolated and that the world depression changed all parameters in a fundamental way. The only idea that was repeatedly put forward was to provide Germany with a long-term loan in exchange for political concessions. But it had always been clear that Brüning was not willing or able to meet French conditions. He would have been immediately removed from office.[12]

One reason for French inertia was their inability to understand the extent of Germany's depression and the ensuing political radicalization. Many French politicians, journalists, and other public figures repeatedly stated that the German government was exaggerating its problems. Even after the disastrous elections that initiated the rise of the Nazi Party, hardliners continued to hold the upper hand. The sense of urgency was not enough to make a difference.[13]

Meanwhile, Hoover was running out of patience. He instructed Treasury Secretary Mellon and Ambassador Edge in Paris to put pressure on Prime Minister Laval and Finance Minister Flandin, while Secretary of State Stimson embarked on a trip to Europe to provide diplomatic support. The Americans and the British asked Germany to make concessions in order to give the Laval cabinet a justification for shifting policy. 'It would be unfortunate, for example, if the impression became general that the Germans are taking everything and giving nothing', the State Department explained to Ambassador Sackett in Berlin. The first response from Berlin was discouraging. But Sackett kept talking to the Chancellor.[14]

Negotiations in Paris started on Saturday, 27 June, and lasted more than a week. The process was enormously complicated and tiresome. Briand regularly fell asleep during the negotiations, and Laval and Flandin kept having to consult the cabinet and outguess the voting behaviour of the parliament. On the other side, Mellon and Edge had to discuss every detail with Washington over the phone. Unfortunately, as the American embassy in Paris was being renovated, the 76-year-old Mellon had to use either the phone in the basement or the phone in the bedroom of Mrs Edge, the wife of the American ambassador. Brüning's reluctance to make concessions further complicated the discussions.[15]

A deal was finally concluded after three things happened. First, Laval waited until parliament went into recess on 4 July so as to have a free hand. This was anything but easy. Some deputies wanted to postpone the adjournment. During heated debates, there were fisticuffs between a right-wing deputy and Laval. Eventually, the Prime Minister won both the physical and political battles.[16]

Second, pressed by the Americans, the German government made a step towards the French. On 2 July, after a series of conversations with Sackett and late evening cabinet meetings, Brüning gave a written statement that 'an increase in the appropriations for the army and navy during the holiday year has never been contemplated nor will it take place'. A few days later, Brüning also agreed to the publication of the statement. It was released on 5 July.[17]

Third, Hoover changed his strategy. By Sunday, 5 July, he had become so annoyed by the French position that he interrupted his stay at his summer residence in Virginia. Upon his arrival in the White House, he told his advisers that 'we did not care what view the French took of our formula; we only wanted yes or no'. Undersecretary of the Treasury Mills vehemently opposed his new tactic, while Senator Reed and Acting Secretary of State Castle endorsed it. Mills went as far as saying that Hoover was 'bringing the would to ruin'. The President went ahead anyway.[18]

By and large, by putting the screws on the French and the German governments, Hoover got what he wanted.[19] The next day, Monday, 6 July, the French government agreed. Hoover's only concession was that Germany formally pay the unconditional annuity to the BIS, and he buried the French proposal that a part of this annuity had to go to Central European countries allied to France. All the money would go to the German railways. Hoover also overturned the French idea that Germany would have to pay the delayed sum as early as the year after the end of the moratorium.

The repayment schedule was much more generous, allowing Germany to pay it back in ten instalments.[20]

When news of the agreement reached Berlin, the joy at the Chancellery was rather subdued. State Secretary Pünder wrote in his diary: 'The Hoover plan has finally been adopted. One would hardly believe it. The negotiations of the last few weeks were dreadful. I have hardly in my life lived such horrible days.'[21]

The reason for Berlin's sober reaction was that Germany's situation had dramatically deteriorated from the moment the French government stopped a rapid adoption of the Hoover plan.[22] On Friday, 26 June, capital outflows resumed (Fig. 9.1). On Saturday, 4 July, two days before the Hoover moratorium was finally adopted, President of the Reichsbank Luther warned Chancellor Brüning that it would be impossible to make the monthly reparations payment due on 15 July if the drain of reserves continued at the same rate.[23]

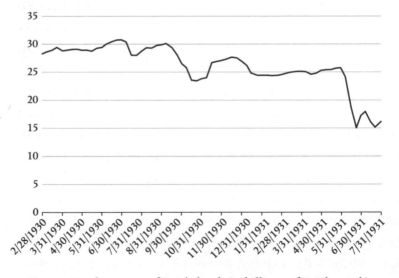

Fig. 9.1 Total reserves of Reichsbank (in billions of Reichsmark)

At this point, nothing was left of the central bank credit of $100 million the Reichsbank had received from the Bank of England, the Banque de France, the Federal Reserve Bank of New York, and the BIS in late June. The central bank credit had been a failure from the beginning, in any case. Instead of lending a huge sum to reassure the markets, the three central banks and the BIS provided only $100 million to be paid back by 16 July. Luther was not even able to keep this disappointingly low amount secret from the press. Confirming that the sum was rather low was a humiliation and reinforced the nervousness of investors instead of easing it. On 5 July, the cover ratio would have dropped below 40 per cent if Luther had not taken the desperate step of transferring an American loan of $50 million which the Gold Discount Bank, a subsidiary of the Reichsbank, had received some time ago to the foreign exchange reserves of the Reichsbank.[24]

In addition, the Brüning cabinet had learnt on 1 July that the losses of Nordwolle amounted to RM 200 million, not RM 54 million as had been officially reported in mid-June. Government officials were shocked by the news. At a cabinet meeting on 4 July, Ernst Trendelenburg, Minister for Economic Affairs, explained what they could expect from a failure of Nordwolle: 'There would be an economic catastrophe, such as we have not experienced for a long time even on the international level.' The government needed to step in if it wanted to prevent Danat Bank, the most important creditor of Nordwolle, from failing. But at this point it was far from clear how to cover the losses. Worse still, one day later, the Berlin correspondent of the Swiss newspaper *National-Zeitung* wrote that one of the great German banks was in difficulties, and the following day, it revealed that it was Danat. Now, everybody knew that Danat was in serious trouble.[25]

Other banks too were on the brink of bankruptcy. On 4 July, a Senator of the City of Bremen informed the government that the Schröder Bank was in trouble. Headquartered in Bremen, the Schröder Bank was, like Danat, closely linked to Nordwolle, which was also headquartered in Bremen. The Rheinische Landesbank continued to be overwhelmed by its mounting problems. In late June, the Reichsbank had been urged to extend a loan, but this provided only temporary relief. On 1 July, the Rheinische Landesbank was forced to stop keeping up with its payments. On 6 July, Brüning revealed the fall of the Rheinische Landesbank in a cabinet meeting, begging his ministers to keep the news secret: 'This exceeds even the case of the "Nordwolle" in terms of volume. Under no circumstances should our fears find their way out of the cabinet.'[26]

What option was left? President of the Reichsbank Luther had two ideas. The first was to form a guarantee syndicate supported by Germany's banks and firms having more than RM 5 million of assets. The syndicate would provide a collateral guarantee of RM 500 million under the leadership of the German Gold Discount Bank, the Reichsbank subsidiary. The syndicate was formed in due time, but failed to stop capital flight.[27]

Luther's second idea was to obtain further credit from foreign central banks. To that end, Luther would fly to London to negotiate with the Bank of England. Governor Montagu Norman tried to discourage him, signalling that he had nothing to offer. But Luther would not take no for an answer and left Berlin on Thursday morning, 9 July. To avoid rumours that would have further undermined the stability of the German currency, he tried to keep his travel secret. His plan worked for the flight from Berlin to Amsterdam, but not for the flight from Amsterdam to London, even though he travelled under a false identity. The London newspapers found out and were waiting for him at noon at Croydon airport. Now, everybody knew that Germany was desperately seeking another foreign bridging credit.[28]

Meanwhile in Berlin, on the same day at noon, Jacob Goldschmidt, head of Danat, came to see the Chancellor to hand over a letter describing the hopeless situation of his bank. From this moment, Brüning held a succession of meetings with ministers, state secretaries, Reichsbank officials, and bankers until midnight. At the end of the day, the Chancellor gathered his closest circle to discuss the options. The consensus was that until Monday evening, there was no reason for concern, as the Reichsbank had the power and the means to provide liquidity to the banking system. But Brüning and his circle had no plan for what would happen after Monday. At that point, they believed, things would have decisively improved thanks to new credit from the Bank of England and other European central banks.[29]

The next morning, Friday, 10 July, Brüning received Luther's message that the Bank of England was opposed to a central bank credit. Luther had met Montagu Norman at Victoria Station, and travelled with him on part of his journey to the BIS meeting that was to take place on Monday in Switzerland. Norman's negative response created an uproar in Berlin. Bernhard von Bülow, State Secretary of the Foreign Ministry, ranted about Luther's failure in a telephone conversation with Schäffer who agreed that the situation had become 'very serious' and that without a central bank credit 'nasty things' would happen. The assumption that the situation could be kept under control proved utterly false.[30]

Luther left Norman at Calais and travelled to Paris to convince French officials to come forward with a central bank credit. As in

London, the press was well informed about Luther's itinerary and laid siege to the Banque de France on Friday morning, 10 July, when he met Governor Moret. The governor was very unhappy about the publicity. Not surprisingly, Moret was against a central bank credit, giving what had become the standard French answer: the German authorities needed to take steps to soothe an anxious and insulted French public and to reassure international financial markets. Luther responded that the central bank credit would have exactly the desired psychological effect, if it was large enough and on a long-term basis. Moret would not budge.[31]

Thereafter, Luther was invited to a lunch with high-ranking French officials at the Hôtel Crillon. Again, the conversation went in circles. First, the French side suggested that the Germans were still living beyond their means. Luther rejected the claim, citing the austerity measures taken by the Brüning government. Finally, the French asked for political action on the German side in order to facilitate cooperation. Finance Minister Flandin, whom Luther met in the afternoon, was also opposed to any unconditional help for Germany. Asked how long Germany would be able to hold its ground, Luther answered that it was not a matter of weeks, but of days. Flandin showed sympathy, but remained non-committal. At the end of his stay in Paris, Luther had another conversation with Governor Moret that ended without palpable result. He then called the Chancellery in Berlin to report that nothing had come out of his visit to Paris.[32]

On Friday evening, 10 July, at the American embassy in Berlin, Schäffer, von Bülow, and Dreyse helped Ambassador Sackett draft a telegram to Hoover. The idea was to bring the White House around to supporting a credit provided by the Federal Reserve Bank of New York to the Reichsbank. Schäffer told Sackett that if there was no positive message from Washington by Sunday morning, at least one big German bank and series of savings banks would have to close their doors on Monday morning and that these moves would probably trigger riots. Von Bülow, known for his hawkish foreign policy stance, went as far as signalling that Germany would be ready to make concessions regarding the customs union and the pocket battleship B, if the White House or the Federal Reserve Bank of New York offered help.[33]

The next day, Saturday, 11 July, Brüning gathered his economic team shortly before noon. Predictably, the situation had further deteriorated. Economics Minister Trendelenburg explained that Danat Bank might collapse over the course of the day, depending on how far share prices dropped. Obtaining a central bank credit from the United States became ever more vital. The cabinet therefore decided to reach out directly to George Harrison, President of the Federal Reserve Bank of New York, and to Parker Gilbert, the former Agent General for Reparations to Germany, who was now an associate at J. P. Morgan. In addition, the Foreign Ministry was authorized to instruct the German ambassadors in London, Paris, Rome, and Washington to draw attention to the grave situation in Germany. The goal was to put on as much pressure as possible to get financial help.[34]

In the afternoon, Danat Bank informed the government that it would not be able to open its doors on Monday. The government also received confirmation that the Rheinische Landesbank had become illiquid. Another emergency meeting was necessary. At 6 p.m., Brüning and the economic team met again, this time with Reichsbank President Luther who had just landed at Tempelhof airport. A senior official of the Reichsbank reported that his telephone conversation with George Harrison of the Federal

Reserve Bank of New York had been entirely pointless. The German government needed to solve its financial and monetary problems by itself.[35]

The economic team then turned to the most pressing issue: the failure of Danat. The crucial question that the Chancellor and his advisers had to answer was how to ring-fence the bank. Brüning was aware of the problem of stigma: once the government publicly singled out Danat as the weakest link, a rescue operation would probably accelerate its bankruptcy which, in a second round, could turn into a full-blown German banking crisis. Economics Minister Trendelenburg sketched three scenarios: one, the Reich would guarantee the credits extended to Danat; two, the Reich would guarantee all Danat's liabilities, possibly in combination with a moratorium; or three, the other big banks would make RM 150 million, backed by the Reich, available to Danat.

An intense discussion followed, with each of the three scenarios finding its proponents. As always, the fickle Chancellor hesitated to take sides, but he believed that the rescue operation had to be supported by finance and industry leaders. Suddenly, the Wilhelmstrasse, which was normally quiet on a Saturday evening, became a hive of activity as one car after another bearing top bankers and industrialists drew up in front of the Chancellery. The meeting began at 9:30 p.m. As the room was overcrowded, the bankers felt uneasy. They had assumed that they could discuss the situation with a couple of cabinet members. Instead they found themselves among about fifty people. And in fact, the discussion was chaotic, with the bankers and experts disagreeing on every issue. Brüning's plan to forge consensus backfired. It ended at 1:15 a.m., and the Chancellor summed it up in two sentences:

'The situation of the banks is worse than expected. We hardly heard any useful suggestions.'[36]

On Sunday, 12 July, 11:50 a.m., Brüning gathered his economic team once again. It was clear to everybody sitting at the table that a solution had to be found before Monday morning. Otherwise, the Danat failure would unleash a banking crisis. State Secretary von Bülow reported that the dominant mood in Washington was that Germany had to help herself. The telegram sent to the White House had completely failed to move the President. Reichsbank President Luther announced that the Reichsbank had begun to ration credit 'in the most severe way' to protect its gold and foreign exchange reserves. This meant that the German banking system would be squeezed by a shortage of liquidity. Economics Minister Trendelenburg protested and advocated a substitute means of payment in order to maintain the economy. Brüning showed sympathy for the idea, but thought the time had not yet come to seriously consider it.[37]

The cabinet was in the midst of considering several ideas to rescue Danat when, unexpectedly, Oscar Wassermann, a managing director of Deutsche Bank, came to the Chancellery to tell Brüning that Dresdner Bank too was about to fail. Obviously, a solution confined to Danat was no longer sufficient. The cabinet had to adopt a broader approach. Brüning requested that the ministries draft an emergency decree authorizing the government to guarantee the deposits of all troubled banks. The meeting ended on 1:50 p.m.[38]

At 4:30 p.m., Brüning summoned the cabinet again. First, it agreed on closing all stock exchanges on Monday and Tuesday. Then, after an extensive discussion, it approved the final wording of the emergency decree and sent it to Neudeck where President

Hindenburg was spending the summer months. The decree consisted of four paragraphs, providing the government with sweeping powers to intervene in the banking system in times of crisis. Finally, the cabinet discussed the regulatory statutes of the decree. It was divided over the question of how high the deposit guarantee should be. Before taking a decision, the ever-hesitant Chancellor wanted again to talk to the banking community. Obviously, the failure to reach a consensus the night before had not dissuaded him from adopting the same approach.[39]

The bankers gathered in the so-called Ländersaal close to the cabinet room. This time nearly a hundred people were there, many more than expected, and the meeting turned out to be even more chaotic than the previous one. Brüning presented the draft of the emergency decree, drawing strong protests from the bankers. They were adamantly against an emergency decree that allowed for government control of all failing banks. Only Danat was having problems, they argued. Brüning retorted: 'Not just the Danat Bank, but also the Dresdner Bank has problems.' Dresdner representatives angrily rejected this claim, but Brüning revealed that he had been informed by Wassermann about Dresdner's dire state, and Wassermann explained that he had been commissioned by the bank to inform the Chancellor. The Dresdner managers repeated their denial, arguing that Wassermann had made it all up. The confusion was total. Brüning got angry, pounding his fist on the table, and criticized the bankers for their behaviour and their lack of clarity. He then went back to the cabinet meeting, telling ministers that the situation had changed once more.[40]

Accepting the declaration by the managers of the Dresdner, the cabinet felt free to concentrate on Danat and agreed on an unlimited guarantee to its foreign and domestic depositors.

At 6:30 p.m., the managing directors of the big banks were invited to the cabinet meeting. Brüning and Economics Minister Trendelenburg informed them about the new rescue plan for Danat. Again, there was disagreement. Wassermann of the Deutsche Bank complained that the draft emergency decree was still aimed at all German banks. It needed to be focused only on Danat, in his view. He also lambasted the Reichsbank for its decision to ration credit: 'These restrictions will mean the destruction of the German credit system.' Luther responded that he had no choice. If he wanted to prevent the cover ratio from falling below the legal minimum of 40 per cent required to maintain the gold standard, he needed to stop providing the banking system with cash and foreign exchange reserves. Before losing control of the debate, the Chancellor told the bankers to hold a separate consultation before coming back to inform him of their conclusions and to provide a clear picture of their institutions' financial situation.[41]

After the bankers left the room, the cabinet continued its discussion. At 9:15 p.m., former Reichsbank President Hjalmar Schacht joined the meeting. Shocked by the magnitude of bank losses and amazed by the 'Babylonian confusion' in the Chancellery, Schacht disagreed with the approach adopted by Brüning. His suggestion was to protect small savers and liquidate Danat without paying the creditors, including foreign ones. In a modern credit system, he argued, it was important that not only the debtor was blamed, but that the creditor equally bore a financial responsibility when losses occurred. Trendelenburg and Schäffer attacked him for being irresponsible, arguing that letting Danat fail would trigger a general bank run. They prevailed.[42]

After this sharp exchange Brüning informed the cabinet that, once more, Dresdner had declared itself solvent and that all bankers wanted at least one bank holiday and still criticized the broad approach of the emergency decree. Luther and Schäffer endorsed the idea of a bank holiday because of time constraints, and the cabinet concurred. With the banking holiday decided, Brüning wanted to address the reservations the bankers had about the emergency decree. For that purpose, the cabinet invited Friedrich Reinhart, managing director of the Commerzbank, to participate in the meeting. Later, other bankers joined the discussion. They still would not accept that the emergency decree should be aimed at the whole German banking sector, and now, surprisingly, they also rejected the idea of a general bank holiday. The argument was that closing Danat would be sufficient to prevent a bank run. The cabinet took notice of their reservations and sent them back to their room.

At 11:15 p.m., the cabinet continued its deliberations. It decided to keep Danat closed on Monday morning and to publish the emergency decree shortly thereafter to provide the necessary legal basis for the intervention of the government. To appease the bankers, the first sentence of the first paragraph of the emergency decree contained the phrase 'in view of the Darmstädter and Nationalbank', thus making it clear that there was no general banking problem in Germany. The cabinet also accepted the bankers' advice to shelve the idea of a general bank holiday. President Hindenburg's office in Neudeck was duly informed that former versions of the decree had become obsolete and the definitive version would be sent the following morning.[43]

After the cabinet had taken all these decisions, Brüning went back to the Ländersaal to inform the bankers. They accepted and went home. Meanwhile, some ministers had left the Chancellery, being convinced that the deal was done. Yet, another cabinet meeting was needed, because it remained unclear how Danat would inform the public about its temporary closure. Goldschmidt, head of Danat, was still in the Chancellery and urged Brüning to allow his bank to put a poster on the doors of its subsidiaries stating that the Reich guaranteed all deposits.[44]

As some ministers had already left, Brüning had to call them back from their beds. Not all of them came back to the Chancellery, however, and those who showed up were disgruntled, especially Finance Minister Dietrich, who could barely compose himself. At 12:40 a.m. the cabinet meeting started, with Luther and Schacht staying on as advisers without a right to vote. Eventually, the cabinet approved the following text: 'The Darmstädter and Nationalbank declares that it is compelled to close its doors on Monday. The Reich Government has authorized the Darmstädter and Nationalbank to issue the following statement: The Government will, under a Presidential emergency decree, to be issued today, guarantee all deposits and liabilities of the bank. In view of these developments it has been proposed that the stock exchange will remain closed today and tomorrow.' Goldschmidt, who was waiting for the final decision in a separate room at the Chancellery, was greatly relieved when receiving the news.[45]

The statement was issued at 3 o'clock in the morning. Meanwhile, Luther made a last attempt to secure a central bank credit. In the middle of the night, he flew to Basle to attend the BIS meeting.[46]

10

THE RISE OF HITLER

Would the measures be sufficient? Initially, the plan seemed to work. On his way to the Chancellery in the morning, State Secretary Hans Schäffer noticed that there were no queues in front of the banks. He talked to passers-by, sensing that people were reacting calmly to the news. When Brüning and his ministers met at 9:30 a.m., they felt that they had taken the right decisions the night before.[1]

Yet, while the cabinet was finalizing the formal part of the rescue operation, a bank run was in the making (Illustration 15). By the hour, one bank after another was confronted with crowds lining up in front of counters and demanding the return of their deposits. From 11:30 a.m. the Berlin banks paid only 20 per cent of what customers demanded, and the Sparkassen introduced a maximum payout of RM 100 per client. The Mayor of Berlin came to the Chancellery to explain that the Berliner Sparkasse had lost RM 7 million and had only RM 1 million left in cash. In Cologne and Hamburg, the banks stopped all payments. The managers of the big banks were so alarmed that they demanded to see the Chancellor, but he declined to receive them. Brüning was angry. He had conceded the night before, trusting their judgement. Now, he let them know that he was busy and that they should talk to senior officials of the Finance Ministry and the Ministry of Economic Affairs. The bankers explained that they were forced to

Illustration 15. Bank run in Berlin on 13 July 1931.

close their branches, 'because otherwise they would not have been able to stand up to the expected storm', and called for two bank holidays—the opposite of what they had asked for one day before.[2]

At 7 p.m., Brüning summoned his economic team. They agreed to declare a general bank holiday and immediately sent the text of an emergency decree to that effect to President Hindenburg in Neudeck. At 10 p.m., after Hindenburg had sent his approval, Brüning gathered all ministers to discuss the regulatory provisions to implement the emergency decree. During the meeting, a senior official of the Reichsbank explained that neither the Bank of England nor the Banque de France nor the Federal Reserve were willing to support Germany with additional funds. Luther's hasty trip to Basle had been a total failure.[3]

At 10:30 p.m., Brüning called the cabinet to a regular meeting to decide on the regulatory provisions. As Germany had not obtained an external lifeline to support the banking system, the cabinet decided that a general bank holiday was to be declared for Tuesday and Wednesday. Brüning ended the meeting with a gloomy speech about the economic prospects and the future of international relations: 'Our misfortune already affects all markets of Europe; the stock exchanges in Warsaw, Riga and Budapest have been closed today, and England also had a black day. The French need to back down and help without setting conditions. If they don't, then something looking entirely different from capitalism will emerge in Europe, and nobody will be more frightened by it than the French.' Hans Schäffer, the State Secretary of the Finance Ministry, wrote in his diary: 'shuddering until 2:30 in the morning'.[4]

Brüning's pessimism was justified. On Tuesday, 14 July, the cabinet heard that Dresdner Bank was about to fail. On Wednesday, 15 July, the cabinet introduced exchange controls to stop capital flight, thus effectively ending the gold standard. Frightened investors began to sell their assets, triggering a global liquidity crisis. In Paris, share prices nosedived. In London, the pound declined by 1 per cent vis-à-vis the French franc, as the Bank of England was confronted with a drain of its reserves. *The Economist* observed that 'the foreign exchange market was thrown into a state of complete chaos'.[5]

In Berlin, the atmosphere suddenly became tense. British ambassador Rumbold observed: 'On my return to Berlin on the 16th July, I was much struck by the emptiness of the streets and the unnatural silence hanging over the city, and particularly by an atmosphere of extreme tension similar in many respects to that which I observed in Berlin in the critical days immediately preceding the war. There was however an essential difference: it was not this time a tension which seemed likely to find expression in action. The predominant note was, and still is, a mixture of almost oriental lethargy and fatalism.'[6]

To be sure, the German government was containing the banking crisis quite well. By early August 1931, payments in the domestic market had been normalized again, and in the following weeks and months the authorities successfully stabilized the financial system. But the rescue required enormous amounts of public funds, while the average citizen was suffering from the depression, so the government could not reap any political credit. More importantly, global contagion could not be stopped, despite frantic diplomatic activity by European governments. On 18 and 19 July, Chancellor Brüning and Foreign Minister Curtius were in Paris to discuss ways out of the debt crisis. From 20 to 23 July, prime, foreign, and finance ministers of Belgium, France, Germany, Great Britain, Italy, Japan, and the United States met in London. But the so-called Seven Powers Conference on German Loans ended inconclusively. The only measure they could agree upon was to commission an experts' committee under the tutelage of the BIS to study the structure of German debt. And they strongly advised banks and bankers not to withdraw their funds from Germany for the time being. The Royal Institute of International Affairs scoffed: 'The London Conference resembled nothing so much as a gathering of fashionable physicians, all anxious above all things to preserve their professional reputations, round the bedside of a prominent patient whose malady they have no genuine hope of curing.'[7]

This pattern was not to change in the following months. Politicians, diplomats, and senior officials were working on a resolution of the crisis, but failed to cut the Gordian knot. The interests of France and Germany could simply not be aligned. In late July 1931, US Secretary of State Stimson as well as British Prime Minister MacDonald and Foreign Secretary Henderson went to Berlin, but returned empty-handed. In late August 1931, the experts' committee commissioned by the Seven Powers Conference published its report on German debts. In mid-September, the so-called stand-still agreement between Germany and its private creditors became effective for six months. In late September 1931, French Prime Minister Pierre Laval and Foreign Minister Aristide Briand went to Berlin for an official visit, and in late October, Laval was in Washington. Shortly before Christmas, the Special Advisory Committee that had been initiated by Germany in accordance with the statutes of the Young Plan published its report named after its chairman, the Italian politician, scholar, and financier Alberto Beneduce. Defying its mandate, the Beneduce report failed to make any recommendations. Diplomacy was back to square one.[8]

The crisis continued to take its course. After Germany, Great Britain was the weakest link in Europe. By the end of July, gold and foreign exchange reserves held by the Bank of England had decreased by almost 20 per cent, and over the course of August, the Bank of England was running out of ammunition to defend the gold standard. To stop the run on the currency, Prime Minister Ramsay MacDonald proposed measures to balance the budget, but the Labour Party declined to follow him. On 24 August, MacDonald, excluded from the Labour Party, formed a so-called National Government gathering Conservatives and Liberals. But the cabinet reshuffle was not enough and, on Saturday, 19 September, the British government declared that it would suspend gold convertibility. Within days, sterling lost more than 20 per cent against the US dollar. Many countries followed, among them Canada, India,

Japan, and the Scandinavian countries. The fall of sterling triggered a run on the US dollar. The Federal Reserve reacted according to the rules of the gold standard by raising the official interest rate from 1.5 to 3.5 per cent. But as the Fed was tightening monetary policy in a deflationary environment, the resulting real interest rate shock triggered another banking crisis and deepened the recession, sending the US unemployment rate above 20 per cent.[9]

The wave of currency devaluations that made Germany's trading partners more competitive and the deterioration of global economic conditions quickly reverberated on the Reich. To lower export costs, Brüning introduced further austerity measures in October and December 1931 through presidential emergency decrees, thus aggravating the German slump in the short term. The alternative, namely to devalue the German currency to the new international level, was rejected because Brüning feared a return of hyperinflation and the inevitable increase in the value of foreign debts denominated in gold. Over the winter months, the number of people unemployed climbed to more than 6 million, according to official figures. According to modern estimates, about 25 per cent of the German workforce was unemployed. In 1932, nearly 40 per cent of industrial workers were without a job. In turn, the continued contraction of the German economy dragged the world economy down further. Over the course of 1931, the GDP of Western Europe shrank by roughly 5 per cent, the US economy by 8 per cent.[10]

It felt like the end of capitalism as people knew it. Looking back at the year 1931, Arnold Toynbee considered it an 'annus terribilis', observing that 'men and women all over the world were seriously contemplating and frankly discussing the possibility that the Western system of society might break down and cease to work'.

Especially the period from May to December 1931 seemed to him 'unlike any months which the living generation of mankind had lived through' since the end of the war. 'To those who lived through those critical months, it felt as though the combined forces of Fate and Folly were making a concentrated attack upon the citadel of civilization.'[11]

Other people rejoiced at the collapse of banks, currencies, and Western values. In Germany, the greatest beneficiary of the financial crisis was Nazi leader Hitler. He managed to monopolize the widespread criticism of the post-war order established by the Versailles Treaty and the Young Plan. Relentlessly, he had made the link between Germany's debt and the economic crisis. His meteoric rise started in the autumn of 1929 when he had been invited by Alfred Hugenberg, the leader of the German National People's Party (DNVP), to join the 'Reich Committee for the German People's Petition Against the Young Plan and the War-Guilt Lie'. Now that the Young Plan was about to collapse under the weight of the German financial crisis, he was in a particularly strong position as he could claim that he had always been right.

Of course, Hitler was not interested in understanding the multidimensional linkages between reparations, foreign short-term debt, financial policy, and economic depression. He was convinced he had a mission that went far beyond the crisis. But he sensed that blaming foreign powers for domestic misery was extremely effective and enjoyed broad support across all parties and all classes in society. Moreover, it was an open secret that the Young Plan in fact constrained Germany's ability to take effective measures against soaring unemployment. Unfortunately, Hitler's criticism had a kernel of truth. Even the Social Democrats became increasingly critical of the Young Plan, as the crisis deepened.[12]

Illustration 16. Adolf Hitler (left) running for the presidency and Joseph Goebbels (right) at a rally in the Lustgarten in Berlin, 4 April 1932.

Obviously, finding an effective message was not the only reason for Hitler's rise. Relative to his competitors within the ranks
of the radical opposition who shared a similar world view, he had
several advantages. Most importantly, he was an able rhetorician
who mesmerized his audiences, whereas the old-fashioned Hugenberg and other leaders of the extreme Right were lacklustre
speakers (Illustration 16). Hitler knew how to play on deep-seated
prejudices, especially anti-Semitic hatred, and to mobilize them for
his political ends. He also seemed to possess an extraordinary stra-
tegic political sense, anticipating developments far in advance and
waiting patiently for an opportunity to outmanoeuvre his opponents. He was anything but an amateur, as many professional

politicians wrongly believed, but an able strategist who successfully deceived his foes and exploited his friends whenever he considered it necessary. Finally, Hitler, a fanatic, was both reckless and
ruthless to an extent that surpassed all conventional barriers,
even in nationalist circles. Consistently, he incited his party members and stormtroopers to use brutal force to intimidate his political
enemies. The end always justified the means. Hitler's personality
played a large part in his and the Nazi Party's success.[13]

But it was the acceleration of the crisis in the summer of 1931
that propelled his party to new heights. Hitler immediately seized
the opportunity to link the country's financial chaos to the Young
Plan. On 14 July 1931, one day after the closing of Danat Bank, he
gave an interview to the United Press International news agency,
in which he reminded the world that he had been right all along.
'The situation as it has developed now has confirmed my former
fears and predictions', he explained. 'The Young plan is ending in
economic disaster. Its consequences will be felt in the whole world,
while the Versailles Treaty, which was made to divide the world
into two parts, will prove a curse on mankind.' As before, he presented his party as the only reliable bulwark against a Bolshevist
takeover: 'There are only two possibilities for the future—either
our movement for power over Bolshevism or Bolshevism, which
is pushing Europe and countries far beyond it into chaos.'[14]

In early August 1931, he repeated his criticism of the Young Plan
in the Nazi press:

> Never in my life have I been as cheerful and pleased as now. For now,
> the eyes of millions of Germans have finally been opened to the hard
> reality, making them see the outrageous trickeries, the outrageous
> lies and the outrageous deceits of the Marxist tricksters. Now the
> broad masses have learned, perhaps for the first time, who was right:
> the Young Plan tricksters of the Social Democrats, of the Centre

Party and the surrounding parties or the men who launched the People's Petition Against the Young Plan. I have therefore rightly felt happy and pleased in recent days, whereas fear and bewilderment have crawled up the necks of the Young front's party and newspaper tricksters.[15]

In October, Hitler intensified his attacks. Brüning was weakened by the resignation of Foreign Minister Curtius and two other members of the cabinet. The Permanent Court of International Justice at The Hague had decided by eight to seven votes that the customs union with Austria promoted by Curtius was incompatible with the Geneva Protocol of 1922 through which Austria had received a major loan in return for renouncing political union with Germany.[16] Moreover, the Reichstag reconvened on 13 October 1931, exposing the Chancellor to a vote of no-confidence. Brüning opened the session to explain the new cabinet's programme but, three days later, the Nazi press published a long 'open letter from Adolf Hitler to the Reich Chancellor' in which, once more, he linked the Young Plan to economic misery.

> Chancellor Brüning, there was a time when you thought that the reparation problem would probably have to be reviewed, but that a practical negotiation would not be possible before the German government had restructured its finances to such an extent that it could appear 'geared up' at the negotiating table. Mister Chancellor! I—and with me all my associates—considered this approach to be false. I was certain that an economic restructuring would be inconceivable without the complete removal of reparations. The idea of gouging out of a people some two or two-and-a-half billion in tributes every year does not lose any of its absurd simplemindedness, when so-called 'economic experts' declare it to be possible or even a good thing.
>
> The fact of the matter is that all the promises and confirmations and assurances made by the camp of the parties whose intellectual heritage you yourself, Mister Chancellor, administer have been downright refuted.

Where are all the commitments, ultimately guaranteed by the Young Plan, concerning the restoration of the finances of the Reich, the Länder and the Communes?

Where is the economic restoration or the stimulation of the economy?

Where has the hereby-reduced number of unemployed been left?

Where are the successes of the 'rescue of agriculture'?

And when, Mister Chancellor Brüning, did the then-promised reduction of taxes finally begin?

Mister Chancellor, you explain in your speech that the failure of all these promises—which has been proven conclusively by today's development—is a 'catastrophe which one could partially foresee, partially not'.

Mister Chancellor Brüning! I may state, to set the historical record straight, that the correct wording of this sentence should be: that we find ourselves in a catastrophe which one part foresaw and another part did not. And I may say, again to set the historical record straight, that I and a series of other party leaders and innumerable other men having both feet on the political and economic ground not only foresaw this catastrophe, but also predicted it precisely![17]

To be sure, the financial crisis did not bring Hitler immediately to power, as some overly optimistic Nazi grandees like Goebbels expected when Danat Bank closed its doors on 13 July. Brüning survived the no-confidence vote in mid-October 1931 and maintained his position until late May 1932 followed by two other chancellors, Franz von Papen and Kurt von Schleicher. Thus, there was no direct road from July 1931 to January 1933 when Hitler was named Chancellor by President Hindenburg. But financial diplomacy failed to contain the crisis and the world economy continued to contract, and the Nazi Party continuously gained ground with the German electorate, especially in bourgeois circles.[18]

Only one month after Hitler's frontal attack against the Chancellor, the Nazi Party began to reap the fruits of its campaigning. At the elections of the People's State of Hesse held on

15 November 1931, it won 37 per cent of the votes, while the Social Democrats, the second largest party, received only 21 per cent. Eighty-two per cent of eligible voters participated. Hessen was a rich state with several industrial districts, so these results showed that the Nazi Party had crushed all bourgeois parties outside of the Catholic milieu. Effectively, only four parties were left: the Nazis, the Centre, the Social Democrats, and the Communists.

In 1932, the Nazi Party reached the same 37 per cent at the April elections in Prussia, a state that held two-thirds of Germany's population. By the time of the national elections in July, Hitler had become the dominant political figure in Germany. True, in the following Reichstag elections in November 1932 the Nazi Party fell back to 33 per cent, but as the Catholic Centre and the Social Democrats lost votes too, the political geometry remained the same. At this point, a Nazi dictatorship was still not inevitable, but neither was it accidental that Hitler would become Chancellor soon thereafter. Debt and a never-ending crisis unleashed forces that were hard to control and turned the worst nightmare into reality.

EPILOGUE

In March 1939, Marcus Wallenberg Sr, the Swedish banker and diplomat, celebrated his seventy-fifth birthday in Stockholm. Among the many well-wishers was Hans Schäffer, the former State Secretary of the German Ministry of Finance. Schäffer had left the Brüning cabinet in mid-May 1932 to become the managing director of Ullstein Verlag, the biggest publishing house in Germany. One year later, he was forced out by Goebbels because of his Jewish background, and eventually, in 1936, moved to Sweden and became a Swedish citizen two years later. He never returned to Germany, even after the first Chancellor of the Federal Republic, Konrad Adenauer, invited him to become State Secretary of the Ministry for Economic Affairs. Born in 1886 in Breslau in the German Empire, he spent the rest of his life in Jönköping where he died in 1967. He was survived by his wife and four daughters.

Schäffer had known Wallenberg since 1924 when they were both involved in the negotiations leading to the Dawes Plan. In 1930 and 1931, they deepened their relationship, as they tried to prevent and contain the financial crisis. Schäffer appreciated the intelligent advice of a neutral financier and introduced him to Brüning. Wallenberg did not act in the name of his country or his bank which made him a credible mediator. In 1933, after being forced out of Ullstein Verlag, Schäffer was offered a job by Wallenberg. The collapse of Ivar Kreuger's match company required enormous legal work, and Schäffer, a lawyer, was asked to help unwind the Kreuger empire. For Schäffer it was 'a gift from heaven', because it allowed him to emigrate and have an income to support his family. Wallenberg also helped Schäffer to obtain Swedish citizenship two years after his arrival. After finishing this task in 1936, Schäffer worked as a legal adviser for the reconstructed match concern.[1]

The gift that Schäffer handed to him in 1939 was a report entitled 'Marcus Wallenberg and the German banking crisis of 1931'. In it, he described how the crisis developed and how Wallenberg advised the Brüning cabinet before and after the fall of Danat Bank. Based on Schäffer's rich diary and an earlier draft on the 'secret history of the banking crisis', the report is one of the best contemporary accounts available. In his introductory words, Schäffer also put the event into the broader historical context. To him, it was evident that Germany's banking crisis had to be analysed from an international, not a domestic perspective.[2]

'The collapse of the biggest German banks in July 1931 represents an essential event in the history of the post-war period. The second year of the Brüning government will have to be considered by a future historian of Germany and Europe with special care. It represented the last attempt to reintegrate Germany into the circle of great powers in an evolutionary way using peaceful means and in a form which did not bear the seed of a future war.'[3]

Schäffer's international perspective is also at the heart of this book. The financial crisis of 1931 occurred because both Germany and its creditors failed to adapt the reparations regime to the rapidly deteriorating domestic economic and political situation. In January 1930 when the Young Plan was agreed upon in The Hague, the gap between the content of the plan and the economic reality on the ground had already widened. Yet, most diplomats and politicians failed to realize that the worldwide recession was not a temporary thunderstorm, but a tsunami that was about to sweep away the financial and monetary foundations of the world economy. And when they slowly began to recognize the extent of the crisis after the parliamentary victory of the Nazi Party in September 1930, they proved unable to cooperate and take clear-eyed, bold action. For its part, the German government, becoming increasingly desperate, came to the conclusion that it needed to question the Young Plan in order to stay in power. Predictably, its manifesto released in early June unleashed a currency crisis which proved impossible to stop, although US President Hoover undertook a last attempt on 20 June. On Monday morning, 13 July, Danat, already weakened by the losses incurred by a major client, closed its doors, and two days later, the German government introduced exchange controls which triggered a global liquidity crisis.

Was there any possibility of adapting the reparations regime in a timely and orderly way? The architects of the Young Plan believed that they had made the necessary provisions. They introduced a clause stating that, if the German government came to the conclusion 'in good faith' that it needed a temporary reduction of reparation payments, the BIS would convene a Special Advisory Committee analysing the German situation and making non-binding recommendations to the creditor governments. In practice, however, this clause proved worthless. For once the German government signalled its inability to transfer the whole annuity, investors would immediately start to withdraw their funds from Germany.

This unworkable clause was symptomatic of the whole process. From the beginning, the victorious powers struggled to make their reparations objectives compatible with economic and political realities in Europe and the United States. Perhaps their post-war interests were simply too divergent to be realigned towards a workable agreement. The situation in 1918–19 was extremely complex and confusing. Yet, the London Ultimatum of 1921 as well as the Dawes Plan of 1924 had deep flaws that narrowed the manoeuvring room of those who tried to avert the financial and political collapse of the Weimar Republic in the early 1930s. The London Ultimatum fixed a stunningly high price that shocked the German public, even though the fine print showed that the effective payment schedule was much less punitive. The Dawes Plan gave the German government an incentive to accumulate foreign debt, with a considerable portion of it short-term. Within five years, the level of foreign debt owed by the Reich to private creditors was almost as high as the reparations bill.

Hans Schäffer's heroic, but ultimately unsuccessful, attempts to navigate through the crisis demonstrates how the debt trap constrained policymakers once the economic crisis took its course. The competent and hard-working State Secretary of the Finance Ministry, who was close to the Social Democrats and the centre-left German Democratic Party (DDP), believed in international cooperation and fully supported the Young Plan. But he knew that fulfilling the Young Plan required that the German government put its financial house in order and wholeheartedly support Brüning's efforts to consolidate the budget. Historians who believe that Germany's policy of retrenchment was a direct consequence of Brüning's conservative and nationalist convictions underestimate the structural constraints. Only the extreme parties were ready to reject the Young Plan and to foster economic growth by expansionary fiscal and monetary policies. Schäffer, by contrast, did not want to risk an abrupt break with the creditor nations. He also believed that Germany was able to meet the conditions of the Young Plan.

Accordingly, it was Schäffer who encouraged the Chancellor in March 1931 to prepare another austerity package in the form of an emergency decree, well knowing that it would have enormous economic and political costs. But he saw no other way to avoid a funding crisis. It was also Schäffer who advised Brüning to combine the publication of the emergency decree with a manifesto signalling that the German people were not willing to make any more sacrifices. 'I like the idea very much', Schäffer noted in his diary. Such a statement, he believed, would enable the government to convey to the domestic audience a willingness to act on reparations without effectively doing something and avoid upsetting foreign diplomats and investors. As we know, this manifesto was the event that triggered the currency crisis in early June 1931. Of course, this was not what Schäffer had intended. Nevertheless, he bore some responsibility.[4]

Schäffer was also one of the architects of the harsh austerity measures of December 1931, known as Fourth Emergency Decree, that pushed the popularity of the Brüning cabinet down to a new low. In fact, Schäffer wanted to go even further than the austere Chancellor, proposing additional taxes to reduce the likelihood of a funding crisis. His failure to prevail contributed to his decision to resign in May 1932. In hindsight, Schäffer was a tragic figure. He invested his talent and influence in a policy that ran counter to his deeply held values. Weakening the Weimar Republic by accelerating the economic crisis was surely not what he had wished for when he became State Secretary of the Finance Ministry in late 1929. Nevertheless, this is what he did because he believed he had no choice.[5]

This raises the question of how the process of concluding international agreements can push well-meaning people to do things which undermine their own democracies and the peaceful cooperation of nations. After the First World War, diplomats and politicians failed to design a reparation framework that balanced rigidity and flexibility in a sustainable way. Once they recognized that the first agreement was dysfunctional, they tried to rescue it by gradually revising it. But this approach proved inadequate, as it did not unmake the initial mistake which consisted of imposing a reparation bill that was simply not enforceable. It may have been just and fair, given what Germany had done during the war, but it proved unrealistic. Thus, in the end, both the creditor nations and German democracy were on the losing side.

Seen from this perspective, the German financial crisis of 1931 appears to be more than a momentous historical episode. Indeed, it is a timeless reminder of the dangers of ignoring the dynamics of domestic politics when setting up international institutions and concluding international agreements. It is not sufficient to have good intentions and appeal to the spirit of cooperation. Nor is it wise to agree on global rules that are not enforceable and then hail them as breakthroughs just because diplomats and politicians are reluctant to return empty-handed after several rounds of contentious and exhausting negotiations. Only when domestic electorates are ready to accept a loss of sovereignty for the benefit of cross-border cooperation can international institutions and agreements have a chance of working effectively and standing the test of time.

NOTES

Introduction

1. (Fröhlich 2005), 56 (14 July 1931).
2. Important contributions are (Balderston 1993), (Bennett 1962), (Borchardt 1991), (Born 1967), (Eichengreen 1992), (Ferguson and Temin 2003), (James 1986), (Ritschl 2002), (Schnabel 2004a). For a research summary see (Burhop 2011), and (James 2013). On the global consequences of the German crisis see (Accominotti 2012), (Ritschl and Sarferaz 2014), and (Straumann, Kugler, and Weber 2017).
3. For a statistical analysis of the negative effects of austerity see (Ponticelli and Voth 2012), (de Bromhead, Eichengreen, and O'Rourke 2013), and (Galofré-Vilà et al. 2017).
4. (Menken 1931), 528. On the tension between international and domestic institutions see (Polanyi 1944), (Eichengreen 2008), (Rodrik 2011), (Bordo and James 2015), and (Temin and Vines 2013). A comparison between the 1930s and the most recent financial crisis is drawn by (James 2009) and (Eichengreen 2015).

Chapter 1: Laughing at the Raven

1. (Somary 1986), 271. See also (James 2009), 75, (Straumann 2013), 9–11, and (Hesse, Köster, and Plumpe 2015), 53, 64.
2. (Somary 1986), 158.
3. (Somary 1932), 45–8.
4. For an overview of the world economic crisis see (Feinstein, Temin, and Toniolo 1997), 171. Total German unemployment: (Balderston 1993), 5 and 9. Comparative industrial employment: (Balderston 2002), 79; real GDP: (Ritschl 2002), 27 and table B.9; GDP per head: The Maddison-Project, <http://www.ggdc.net/maddison/maddison-project/home.htm> (2013 version).
5. (Somary 1986), 104.
6. (Mertz-Rychner 1991), 98; (Somary 1994), 9.

7. *The Economist*, 12 November 1932: War Debts supplement, 4. Cf. (James 2014), 278.
8. (Ritschl 2013), 116. Cf. (Schuker 1988), 49.
9. (Bähr and Rudolph 2011), 32; (Borchardt 1991), 157; (James 1986), 42 and 49; (Feldman 1993), 837.
10. The senior official was Hans Simon. Quoted in (Heyde 1998), 38. Cf. (Bennett 1962), 7–8, (Ritschl 2002), 120–41, and (James 2014), 279.
11. (Bähr and Rudolph 2011), 32.
12. (Bähr and Rudolph 2011), 32; (Balderston 2002), 10–14.
13. J. Morgan to T. Lamont, 30 August 1929, quoted in (James 1985), 111. For a description of the lending frenzy see (James 2014), 48–50, and (Eichengreen 2015), 54–9.
14. (Kindleberger 1973), 56 (table 1), 71 (table 2); (McNeil 1986), 218; (Wolf 2010), 349.
15. (Leith-Ross 1968), 102 (footnote 1); ADAP, Serie B, Volume VII, 244. Parker Gilbert's first warning to the German government was expressed in a memorandum in October 1927.
16. (Enquête-Ausschuss 1929), 164ff. On Schacht's controversial attempt to stop the stock market boom and slow down capital inflows see (Voth 2003).
17. (Somary 1932), 45, 71; (Somary 1986), 158.
18. *Le Figaro* quoted in and translated in (Shamir 1989), 33; portrait of de Margerie in (Shamir 1989), 52.
19. (Johnson and Moggridge 1978), 2–3.
20. (Somary 1986), 146–7.
21. (Somary 1986), 150–1.
22. (Somary 1986), 156.

Chapter 2: A Triumph of Diplomacy

1. *Petit Parisien*, 21 January 1930, 1; *The Times*, 21 January 1930, 14; NYT, 21 January 1930, 6; VZ, 21 January 1930, morning edition, 1.
2. *The Times*, 21 January 1930, 14; VZ, 2 January 1930, morning edition, 1. On Snowden's bad reputation during the conference see (Schäffer 1967), 56, and (Curtius 1950), 72.
3. *The Times*, 22 January 1930, 15; *The Economist*, 25 January 1930, 163; NYT, 22 January 1930, 22.
4. *Le Temps*, 22 January 1930, 1 (editorial).
5. (Curtius 1948), 90; VZ, 3 October 1929, evening edition, 1.

6. (Unger 2005), 559–60; (Schäffer 1967), 63–4.

7. (Knipping 1987), 9–31; (Kolb 2003), 94–7.

8. (Unger 2005), 17–20; (Kolb 2003), 9; (Schwerin-Krosigk 1951), 76.

9. Ernst von Weizsäcker quoted in (Rödder 1996), 41; (Tabouis 1958), 68.

10. On the continuity of German foreign policy from Stresemann to Curtius see (Heyde 1998), 56. On Tardieu's career and political thinking see (Monnet 1993).

11. (Unger 2005), 564–5.

12. (Curtius 1948), 122; (Leith-Ross 1968), 127.

13. *The Economist*, 25 January 1930, 162; VZ, 20 January 1930, morning edition, 1; (Schmidt 1949), 193.

14. *The Times*, 21 January 1930, 14; quote of the French delegation in (Rödder 1996), 65.

15. For a review of reparation agreements see (Marks 1978), (Gomes 2010), and (Ritschl 2013). For an analysis of the Versailles Treaty see (MacMillan 2001), (Tooze 2014), and (Kershaw 2015).

16. This is the main thesis of (Kindleberger 1973) and (Temin and Vines 2013).

17. On the economic burden of reparations see (Hantke and Spoerer 2010) and (Ritschl 2013). (Holtfrerich 1986) and (Feldman 1993) are the standard references for the German hyperinflation.

18. (Zweig 2013), chapter 15.

19. (Balderston 2002), 53–8, and (Wehler 2003), 247–9.

20. (Kindleberger 1973), 38 and 54; (James 1986), 48; (Feinstein, Temin, and Toniolo 1997), 91 (table 5.2); (Ritschl 2002), 228.

21. (Leith-Ross 1968), 102.

22. This argument has mainly been put forward by (Ritschl 2002). For a shorter version see (Ritschl 2013).

23. See Chapter 1 ('Laughing at the Raven'): (Somary 1932), 46. For an analysis of capital ratios of the German banking system see (Schnabel 2004a), 839, and (Eichengreen 2015), 138.

24. (Moulton and Pasvolsky 1932), 223ff.

25. Owen Young quoted in (Link 1970), 489.

26. (Curtius 1948), 138–41.

27. (Maurer, Wengst, and Heideking 1980), 206; (Schuker 1988), 47–8; (Wandel 1974), 127, 145; (James 1985), 109 (footnote 45); (Schäffer 1967), 48.

28. (Somary 1986), 155, 157–8, 163.

29. (Bachmann 1996), 127ff. and 153; (Maurer 1973), 48ff. and 65; (Somary 1986), 155–6.

Chapter 3: 'Strong Cards to Play'

1. Votes by Reichrat: Young Plan: 42 yes, 5 no; Polish agreement: 30 yes, 10 no.
2. VZ, 13 March 1930, morning edition, 1.
3. VZ, 12 March 1930, evening edition, 1.
4. Verhandlungen des Reichstags, 12 March 1930, 4364: Löbe (SPD, President of Reichstag), 4388: Gregor Strasser (NSDAP).
5. Verhandlungen des Reichstags, 12 March 1930, 4368–9: Max Wallraf (DNVP).
6. (Kershaw 1999), 310.
7. Verhandlungen des Reichstags, 12 March 1930, 4391: Walter Stoecker (KPD).
8. Verhandlungen des Reichstags, 12 March 1930, 4363; (Maurer 1973), 120–1; (Pünder 1961), 43.
9. Le Temps, 14 March 1930, 1 (bulletin du jour).
10. (Pyta 2007), 461 and 545–53.
11. AdR, Müller II, 1544 and 1580–2; (Curtius 1948), 143.
12. (Winkler 2000), 458ff. and 485–7; (Wehler 2003), 350f.; (Pyta 2007), 557.
13. (Wandel 1974), 141. Cf. portrait of Schleicher by (Meissner 1950), 256.
14. (James 1986), 52; (Brown 1988), 229; (Balderston 1993), 1, 5; (Balderston 2002), 77, 270; (Ritschl 2002), Appendix Table B.1.
15. (Maurer 1973), 49; (Wandel 1974), 138; (Bachmann 1996), 127. Unemployment figures in (Balderston 1993), 2.
16. (Pünder 1961), 45–6 (Kindleberger 1973), 139; (Maurer, Wengst, and Heideking 1980), 100; (Winkler 2000), 488; (Evans 2003), 247. (Winkler 2000), 487; (Pyta 2007), 552–3.
17. Two excellent biographies are (Patch 1998) and (Hömig 2000). See also (Hömig 2000), 18–19 and 22–6, for a survey of biographies and varying assessments of Brüning's chancellorship by historians.
18. (Maurer, Wengst, and Heideking 1980), 100–1.
19. (Patch 1998), 23.
20. (Schwerin-Krosigk 1951), 131; (Lohe 1961), 115; (Luther 1964), 114; (Burke 1994), 99; (Patch 1998), 23; (Hömig 2000), 22 and 211ff.
21. (Schwerin von Krosigk 1974), 64.
22. (Treviranus 1968), 117.
23. VZ, 30 March 1930, 1; (Pünder 1961), 46.
24. (Winkler 2000), 487–8.
25. (Maurer 1973), 141; (Schwerin von Krosigk 1974), 60–1.
26. VZ, 28 March 1930, evening edition, 6; Financial Times quoted in (Brown 1988), 235.

27. NYT, 29 March 1930; *The Times*, 29 March 1930; *The Times*, 31 March 1930; *The Economist*, 5 April 1930, 766.
28. *Le Temps*, 4 April 1930, 1 (bulletin du jour); *L'Œuvre*, 1 April 1930, 1, quoted in (Brüning 2010), 152–3; *Le Parisien*, 28 March 1930, 1; *Le Parisien*, 29 March 1930, 1.
29. *Le Figaro*, 29 March 1930. Cf. (Brüning 2010), 155.
30. (Pünder 1961), 50–1.
31. (Maurer, Wengst, and Heideking 1980), 206; (Bachmann 1996), 196–9.
32. (Mouré 1991), 14–16.
33. Survey of International Affairs 1930, 136–7; (Tabouis 1958), 64.
34. *Federal Reserve Bulletin*, May 1930, 285; Herbert Hoover, 'The President's News Conference', 7 March 1930. Online by Gerhard Peters and John T. Woolley, *The American Presidency Project*. <http://www.presidency.ucsb.edu/ws/?pid=22539>. See also (Kindleberger 1973), 128.
35. NYT, 8 March 1930, 1. (Rappleye 2016), 115, highlights Hoover's communication difficulties. For a positive view of Hoover by today's historians see (Crafts and Fearon 2010), 293.

Chapter 4: Hitler's Victory

1. NYT, 30 June 1930, 1.
2. *The Economist*, 21 June 1930, 1378. For the modern view on the Smoot–Hawley Tariff Act see (Irwin 2011).
3. (Brüning 1970), 170; (Knipping 1987), 57; (Heyde 1998), 50; DBFP 1919–39, Second Series, Volume 1, 475–6.
4. DBFP 1919–39, Second Series, Volume 1, 487–8. Original text printed in VZ, 1 July 1930, morning edition, 1.
5. NYT, 1 July 1930, 1 and 13.
6. AdR, Brüning I, 199.
7. *Le Temps*, 2 July 1930, 1 (bulletin du jour); DBFP 1919–39, Second Series, Volume 1, 486.
8. Printed in NYT, 2 July 1930; VZ, 3 July 1930, evening edition, 1; VZ, 4 July 1930, evening edition, 1.
9. *Le Temps*, 7 July 1930, 1 (bulletin du jour); (Shamir 1989), 15 and 17.
10. DBFP 1919–39, Second Series, Volume 1, 598–603.
11. ADAP, Serie B, Volume XV, 299–305. Cf. (Heyde 1998), 88.
12. AdR, Brüning I, 87; (Brüning 1970), 177.
13. Survey of International Affairs, 1930: The Briand Plan for Closer Union in Europe, 131–42; (Knipping 1987), 225; (Heyde 1998), 84, 89–90. Cf. AdR, Brüning I, 281.

14. (Kindleberger 1973), 128; (Toniolo 2005), S. 71–2; *Der Deutsche Volkswirt*, 4 July 1930, Nr. 40, 4. Jg., 1361f., quoted in (Bachmann 1996), 204.
15. (Maurer, Wengst, and Heideking 1980), 207; Schäffer, Diary, 10 May 1930.
16. VZ, 6 June 1930, evening edition, 1–2. Cf. AdR, Brüning I, 192.
17. *Vorwärts*, 6 June 1930, morning edition, 1; (Maurer, Wengst, and Heideking 1980), 243–6; AdR, Brüning I, 211–12.
18. The new Minister for Economic Affairs was Trendelenburg.
19. (Treviranus 1968), 28–9; (Schwerin von Krosigk 1974), 62–3; (Wandel 1974), 150.
20. Schäffer, Diary, 24 June 1930.
21. Verhandlungen des Reichstags, 16 July 1930, 6407; final result: 6435 (256 no, 193 yes).
22. *Vorwärts*, 17 July 1930, 1; Verhandlungen des Reichstags, 18 July 1930, 6523: Communists.
23. AdR, Brüning I, 329–30; VZ, 27 July 1930, evening edition, 1. Cf. (Bachmann 1996), 201; (Patch 1998), 95.
24. (Curtius 1948), 164; (Hömig 2000), 177; VZ, 19 July 1930, morning edition, 1.
25. (Winkler 2000), 490; (Schulz 1992), 118; (Patch 1998), 94–5; (Hömig 2000), 185; (Kershaw 1999), 412, disagrees; AdR, Brüning I, 321.
26. (Hömig 2000), 171. Cf. (Brüning 1970), 182.
27. *Der Deutsche Volkswirt*, 5 September 1930, Beilage No. 49, 766, quoted in (Brown 1988), 241.
28. *The Economist*, 26 July 1930, 170, 176; *The Times*, 21 July 1930, 13; *Le Temps*, 14 July 1930, 1 (bulletin du jour).
29. Quoted in (Shamir 1989), 22 and 52–3.
30. The German ambassador in Paris, Leopold von Hoesch, was exactly right when he explained the French state of mind to his superiors in Berlin: ADAP, Serie B, Volume XV, 383 and 385–7.
31. (Maurer, Wengst, and Heideking 1980), 357; DBFP 1919–39, Second Series, Volume 1, 505; (Pünder 1961), 58–9.
32. (Pünder 1961), 59–60; VZ, 15 September 1930, evening edition, 1.
33. (Wandel 1974), 154.
34. Hitler: Reden, Schriften, Anordnungen: Februar 1925 bis Januar 1933, Band III, Teil 3: Rede auf NSDAP-Versammlung in München, 18 July 1930, 279.
35. Hitler: Reden, Schriften, Anordnungen: Februar 1925 bis Januar 1933, Band III, Teil 3: Rede auf NSDAP-Führertagung in München, 27 July 1930, 291–2.
36. (Heyde 1998), 91; (Patch 1998), 102 and 130–1; (Schulz 1992), 123; (Kershaw 1999), 330; (Evans 2003), 218; (Herbert 2014), 280.

37. AdR, Brüning I, 385.
38. *Le Temps*, 15 September 1930, 1.
39. (Evans 2003), 261–5; (Herbert 2014), 285–6.
40. VZ, 15 September 1930, evening edition, 2.
41. (Fröhlich 2005), 239 (15 September 1930).

Chapter 5: To the Brink and Back

1. (Maurer, Wengst, and Heideking 1980), 383–6.
2. (Curtius 1948), 171.
3. (Pünder 1961), 60.
4. (Maurer, Wengst, and Heideking 1980), 385; AdR, Brüning I, 429.
5. AdR, Brüning I, 430.
6. VZ, evening edition,15 September 1930.
7. VZ, evening edition, 16 September 1930; (Brown 1988), 241.
8. AdR, Brüning I, 434 (footnote 2); (Heyde 1998), 95; VZ, 20 September 1930, evening edition, 1; VZ, 19 September 1930, evening edition, 5; NYT, 20 September 1930, 7.
9. AdR, Brüning I, 432–4; (Maurer, Wengst, and Heideking 1980), 397–400.
10. (Heyde 1998), 61.
11. (Maurer, Wengst, and Heideking 1980), 379; AdR, Brüning I, 432–4; (Bennett 1962), 17.
12. Cf. biography by (Partnoy 2009).
13. AdR, Brüning I, 434; (Brown 1988), 244; VZ, 20 September 1930, morning edition, 5.
14. AdR, Brüning I, 447–9; VZ, 25 September 1930, evening edition, 5; VZ, 26 September 1930, morning edition, 14.
15. Schäffer, Diary, 26 September 1930; (Bachmann 1996), 213; AdR, Brüning I, 480–1.
16. Schäffer, Diary, 28 September 1930; all questions and answers are listed in AdR, Brüning I, No. 127; AdR, Brüning I, 502 (footnote 2); (Heyde 1998), 95, 125.
17. AdR, Brüning I, 498; Schäffer, Diary, 2 October 1930. Cf. Schäffer, Diary, 1 October 1930: Krosigk tells Schäffer about the treasuries.
18. AdR, Brüning I, 498–504. Cf. Schäffer, Diary, 2 October and 5 October 1930.
19. AdR, Brüning I, 502–3 (see also 504: 'Anlage'); Schäffer, Diary, 6 October 1930.
20. (Pünder 1961), 61–2. See AdR, Brüning I, 470–5, for a complete list. Cf. (Wandel 1974), 154.

21. AdR, Brüning I, 469; (Wandel 1974), 154; Schäffer, Diary, 1 October 1930; VZ, 1 October 1930, morning edition, 2; (Pünder 1961), 64.
22. VZ, 7 October 1930, morning edition, 1–2.
23. (Fröhlich 2005), 255 (6 October 1930). Later sources report that Hitler had an inferiority complex towards Brüning: (Patch 1998), 136.
24. (Brüning 1970), 191–6; (Treviranus 1968), 162.
25. For a critical assessment of Brüning's memoirs see (Morsey 1975), (Hömig 2000), 20–2; (Patch 1998), 135.
26. AdR, Brüning I, 511.
27. Schäffer, Diary, 8 October 1930; VZ, 9 October 1930, evening edition, 1.
28. See the biography by (Kopper 2006).
29. (Wala 2001), 161–2; Schäffer, Diary, 1 October 1930; NYT, 3 October 1930: Notes of Social Activities in New York and Elsewhere.
30. (Schacht 1953), 342; NYT, 3 October 1930.
31. NYT, 4 October 1930, 8. Cf. (Heyde 1998), 101.
32. VZ, 7 October 1930, evening edition, 2; (Brüning 1970), 197; VZ, 10 October 1930, morning edition, 1.
33. Schäffer, Diary, 10 October and 14 October 1930.
34. Schäffer, Diary, 11 October 1930; (Bennett 1962), 19; (Bachmann 1996), 218.
35. Schäffer, Diary, 10 October 1930; VZ, 12 October 1930, Sunday edition, 1; (Pünder 1961), 67.
36. VZ, 14 October 1930, evening edition, 1; (Brüning 1970), 199; (Heyde 1998), 96; VZ, 14 October 1930, morning edition, 2.
37. VZ, 14 October 1930, morning edition, 2.
38. VZ, 14 October 1930, morning edition, 5; VZ, 14 October 1930, evening edition, 2.
39. VZ, 15 October 1930, morning edition, 1; VZ, 15 October 1930, evening edition, 1; VZ, 16 October 1930, evening edition, 1. Cf. (Brüning 1970), 199–200.
40. Verhandlungen des Reichstags, 18 October 1930, 112–201; VZ, 19 October 1930, evening edition, 1.
41. (Pünder 1961), 67; VZ, 19 October 1930, evening edition, 1; (Hardach 1976), 121; (Brüning 1970), 201.

Chapter 6: 'The First Real Chancellor Since Bismarck'

1. *The Times*, 21 October, 1930, 14; (Brown 1988), 246; VZ, 18 November 1930, evening edition, Finanz- und Handelsblatt der Vossischen Zeitung. Cf. (Hardach 1976), 121.
2. AdR, Brüning I, 509.

3. Hitler, *Sunday Express*, 28 September 1930, in Hitler: Schriften, Reden, Anordnungen: Band III, Teil 3, 455.
4. (Maurer, Wengst, and Heideking 1980), 417–19.
5. (Heyde 1998), 125; (Eichengreen 2015), 136.
6. *Le Temps*, 16 September 1930, 1; *Le Figaro*, 16 September 1930, 1.
7. (Bennett 1962), 17; (Heyde 1998), 135; (Maurer, Wengst, and Heideking 1980), 400–1.
8. (Shamir 1989), 5–7; (Eichengreen 2015), 134–46.
9. *The Times*, 16 September 1930, 13 (editorial); *The Economist*, 20 September 1930, 512; (Brown 1988), 242. Cf. *The Economist*, 4 October 1930, 620–1.
10. DBFP 1919–39, Second Series, Volume 1, 525–27, 535, 537. Cf. (Bennett 1962), 26ff., on British demarche on 10 December, 1930.
11. NYT, 16 September 1930, 3 and 20 (editorial).
12. (Wicker 1996), 24ff.
13. NYT, 19 October 1930, 36; FRUS, 1930, Volume 3, 89.
14. (Somary 1931).
15. (Somary 1986), 162.
16. Schäffer, Diary, 15 December 1930.
17. AdR, Brüning I, 728–9.
18. AdR, Brüning I, 755–8.
19. (Fromm 1990), 24 and 28. Cf. portrait of Sackett in VZ, 20 January 1930, evening edition, 1.
20. (Bennett 1962), 31; AdR, Brüning I, 757–8.
21. Stimson, Diary, 10 October 1930 and 28 December 1930, quoted in (Link 1970), 499. Cf. (Link 1970), 505.
22. NYT, 12 January 1931, 1.
23. NYT, 16 January 1931, 1.
24. NYT, 12 January 1931, 1, and 16 January 1931, 1; (Bennett 1962), 38.
25. *Chicago Tribune*, 10 March, 1931, 22; (Burke 1994), 112; (Bennett 1962), 37.
26. (Brüning 1970), 230; (Hardach 1976), 123; (Link 1970), 492; AdR, Brüning I, 855 (footnote 2) and 856–7.
27. (Bachmann 1996), 235ff.; (Burke 1994), 115; (Ferguson and Temin 2003), 13; (Schulz 1992), 294ff.; VZ, 9 February 1931, evening edition, 1; NYT, 17 February 1931, 8.
28. (Brown 1988), 247; (Heyde 1998), 119; (Hardach 1976), 123–4; (Wandel 1974), 169; NYT, 12 January 1931, 1.
29. (Schulz 1992), 282–3; (Rödder 1996), 92; DBFP 1919–39, Second Series, Volume 1, 559.
30. NYT, 12 January 1931, 1; (Bennett 1962), 123.
31. DBFP 1919–39, Second Series, Volume 1, 577–8 and 580.

32. AdR, Brüning I, 963 (footnote 6); AdR, Brüning I, 1018 (footnote 5); Cf. (Heyde 1998), 167–9; (Curtius 1948), 213; *The Times*, 5 June 1931, 15 (editorial).
33. *NYT*, 14 February 1931, 9.
34. (Schäffer 2008), 23.
35. (Rödder 1996), 122. Cf. (Bennett 1962), 93.

Chapter 7: Squaring the Circle

1. AdR, Brüning I, 926–7. Cf. (Patch 1998), 150.
2. (Pünder 1961), 93.
3. AdR, Brüning I, 970–1.
4. VZ, 20 March 1931, evening edition, 1; *The Times*, Saturday, 21 March 1931; 11. ADAP, Serie B, Band XVII, 93–6. The precise chronology is described in (Rödder 1996), 202–3.
5. *Le Temps*, 23 March 1931, 1 (editorial); *Le Petit Parisien*, 29 March 1931, 1; *NYT*, 23 March 1931, 2.
6. FRUS, 1931, Volume 1, 590. The standard story highlights the article published by the *Neue Freie Presse* (Vienna) on 17 March 1931. But according to (Bennett 1962), 58, and (Hömig 2000), 299, the French knew about it a few days earlier.
7. (Curtius 1948), 195; (Knipping 1987), 215; *The Times*, 25 March 1931, 14; (Rödder 1996), 205–6; DBFP, 1919–39, Second Series, Volume 2, 12–14. AdR, Brüning I, 984–6; *NYT*, 25 March 1931. Cf. FRUS, 1931, Volume 1, 572ff.
8. AdR, Brüning I, 970; (Hömig 2000), 296; Vansittart quoted in (Rödder 1996), 200 (footnote 91).
9. AdR, Brüning I, 970.
10. (Brüning 1970), 263–70. Cf. (Hömig 2000), 302, is also critical of Brüning's indecision regarding the plan.
11. *NYT*, 1 April 1931.
12. (Balderston 1993), 5; *Der deutsche Volkswirt*, Die Konjunktur, 3 April 1931; VZ, 17 April 1931, evening edition, 7; Sackett quoted in (Ferguson and Temin 2003), 39.
13. (Büttner 2008), 421; (Patch 1998), 147; VZ, 27 March 1931, morning edition, 1; (Evans 2003), 269–70; (Pünder 1961), 94.
14. (Fröhlich 2005), 376 (1 April 1931); (Burke 1994), 160ff.; (Fröhlich 2005), 378 (4 April 1931).
15. (Knortz 2010), 247; German Medical Association quoted in *NYT*, 20 June 1931, 8; *Freie Welt* quoted by (Herbert 2014), 265.
16. AdR, Brüning I, 1043; AdR, Brüning I, 1053.
17. AdR, Brüning I, 1054–7.

18. AdR, Brüning I, 1962–3; Schäffer, Diary, 11 May and 12 May 1931; (Schubert 1991), 10; (Macher 2015), 12–15. The Austrian crisis had little impact on German banks: (Schnabel 2004a), 852; (Hardach 1976), (James 1984), (Ferguson and Temin 2003), and (Burhop 2011), 20–1.
19. Quoted in (Leith-Ross 1968), 133.
20. (Schubert 1991), 12; (Marcus 2011), 302 and 306.
21. *Neue Freie Presse*, 29 May 1931, morning edition, 1.
22. VZ, 12 May 1931, evening edition, 5; Schäffer, 12 May 1931.
23. VZ, 9 May 1931, morning edition, 1.
24. The SPD, the DDP, and the DVP lost 8 per cent, 7.5 per cent and 13.6 per cent respectively. The turnout was high: 75 per cent against 70 per cent in the last elections of May 1928. (Fröhlich 2005), 409 (19 May 1931); (Maurer, Wengst, and Heideking 1980), 623–7, quote on 626; AdR, Brüning I, 1140–2; (Heyde 1998), 173. On 26 May, the Brüning cabinet discussed a rescue package for Vienna: AdR, Brüning I, 1104–6.
25. VZ, 19 May 1931, evening edition, 1–2; Le Temps, 1 June 1931, editorial, 1; VZ, 11 June 1931, evening edition, 1. Cf. (Brüning 1970), 272–3.
26. AdR, Brüning I, 1147. Cf. (Maurer, Wengst, and Heideking 1980), 632–6.
27. AdR, Brüning I, 1171 and 1178; (Schwerin von Krosigk 1974), 68. Cf. (Pünder 1961), 98.
28. AdR, Brüning I, 1178; (Brüning 1970), 278; (Pünder 1961), 98; *The Times*, 4 June 1931, 14; *The Times*, 5 June 1931, 15.
29. (Schmidt 1949), 201–3; (Brüning 1970), 278.
30. *The Times*, 5 June 1931, 14; *The Times*, Saturday, 6 June 1931, 12.
31. *The Times*, Saturday, 6 June 1931, 15; (Brüning 1970), 279.
32. (Brüning 1970), 279; Schäffer, Diary, 5 June 1931; AdR, Brüning I, 1183.
33. (Brüning 1970), 279–81.
34. (Schmidt 1949), 205; FRUS 1931, Volume 1, 007, General, 10.
35. (Brüning 1970), 281; (Leith-Ross 1968), 134; DFBP 1919–39, Second Series, Volume 2, 71–7. Cf. (Schmidt 1949), 205–6.
36. DFBP 1919–39, Second Series, Volume 2, 71–7; (Maurer, Wengst, and Heideking 1980), 650.
37. DBFP 1919–39, Second Series, Volume 2, 74. Cf. (Schmidt 1949), 209.
38. (Toniolo 2005), 88–97.
39. DBFP 1919–39, Second Series, Volume 2, 76.
40. (Bennett 1962), 128; *The Sunday Times* (London), Sunday, 7 June 1931, 15.
41. DBFP 1919–39, Second Series, Volume 2, 77; (Brüning 1970), 283.
42. (Brüning 1970), 284.
43. (Schmidt 1949), 213–14; (Bennett 1962), 141–2; (Pünder 1961), 99.
44. (Heyde 1998), 189; (Schmidt 1949), 214–15.

Chapter 8: Help from Washington

1. (James 1986), 302; VZ, 9 June 1931, evening edition, 5; (Priester 1932), 23.
2. (Priester 1932), 22–3; (Born 1967), 71; VZ, 5 June 1931, evening edition, 5.
3. See the debate between I. Schnabel and T. Ferguson/P. Temin: (Schnabel 2004a), (Ferguson and Temin 2004), and (Schnabel 2004b).
4. (Feldman 1994), 316.
5. (Born 1967), 96–7; (Feldman 1994), 318; (James 1986), 310; (Bähr and Rudolph 2011), 48.
6. (James 2013), 122; (Feldman 1994), 324.
7. (Eichengreen 2015), 144.
8. (Pünder 1961), 99; (Hardach 1976), 128; AdR, Brüning I, 1189 and 1190–1; (Maurer, Wengst, and Heideking 1980), 653 (footnote 17). Cf. VZ, 12 June 1931, morning edition, 1.
9. (Hömig 2000), 277; VZ, 12 June 1931, evening edition, 3.
10. AdR, Brüning I, 1191 (footnote 1); (Brüning 1970), 286–7.
11. (Priester 1932), 24; (Born 1967), 73; (Fröhlich 2004), 37 (13 June 1931).
12. (Pünder 1961), 100; AdR, Brüning I, 1214 (footnote 6).
13. AdR, Brüning I, 1198–204; (Pünder 1961), 100.
14. VZ, 16 June 1931, evening edition, 1; AdR, Brüning I, 1212 and 1214 (footnote 6).
15. (Pünder 1961), 100.
16. (Luther 1964), 170; (Born 1967), 76–7; (Priester 1932), 31.
17. The correct name is Landesbank of the Rheinprovinz. VZ, 18 June 1931, evening edition, 5; (Bähr and Rudolph 2011), 72; AdR, Brüning I, 1295–6 and 1298–300; (Burhop 2011), 15.
18. (Bähr and Rudolph 2011), 41; Schäffer, Diary, 19 June 1931; The Economist, 20 June 1931.
19. VZ, 20 June 1931, morning edition, 1; Herbert Hoover: 'Statement About Conferences on the Economic Situation in Germany.' 19 June 1931. Online by Gerhard Peters and John T. Woolley, The American Presidency Project. <http://www.presidency.ucsb.edu/ws/?pid=22717>.
20. Schäffer, Diary, 20 June 1931.
21. The exact time is drawn from (Brüning 1970), 292.
22. (Pünder 1961), 101; (Heyde 1998), 195; DBFP 1919–39, Second Series, Volume 2, 85–6; (Brüning 1970), 292; FRUS 1931, Volume 1, 39; Schäffer, Diary, 20 June 1931.
23. FRUS 1931, Volume 1, 32–9; (Brüning 1970), 292; Schäffer, Diary, 20 June 1931; (Pünder 1961), 101.
24. FRUS, 1931, Volume 1, 33; Herbert Hoover: 'Statement Announcing the Proposal of the Moratorium on Intergovernmental Debts', 21 June 1931.

Online by Gerhard Peters and John T. Woolley, *The American Presidency Project*. <http://www.presidency.ucsb.edu/ws/?pid=22720>.

25. Herbert Hoover: 'Statement Announcing the Proposal of the Moratorium on Intergovernmental Debts', 21 June 1931. Online by Gerhard Peters and John T. Woolley, *The American Presidency Project*. <http://www.presidency.ucsb.edu/ws/?pid=22720>.

26. (Bennett 1962), 136; (Rappleye 2016), 188.

27. Herbert Hoover, Public Papers, 1931: containing the public messages, speeches, and statements of the president, 1 January to 31 December 1931, 657–8; (Burke 1994), 127.

28. Hoover, Public Papers, Volume 2, 1931, 659.

29. (Heyde 1998), 170; Hoover, Public Papers, Volume 2, 1931, Supplement I, 658–9.

30. Stimson, Diary, 13 July 1931, quoted in (Rappleye 2016), 257–9; Hoover, Public Papers, 1931, Volume 2, Supplement I, 662.

31. NYT, 11 June 1931, 2.

32. Hoover, Public Papers, Volume 2, 1931, Supplement I, 668. (14 June 1931)

33. FRUS, 1931, Volume 1, 19; Hoover, Memoirs, Volume 3, 68; (Schäffer 2008), 31–2; Stimson, Diary, 19 June 1931, quoted in (Wala 2001), 174.

34. (Priester 1932), 31.

35. NYT, 22 June 1931, 15; *The Times*, 22 June 1931, 13.

36. Speech of Brüning on 23 June 1931. English version in FRUS, 1931, Volume 1, 51.

37. (Fröhlich 2004), 44 (24 June 1931).

Chapter 9: Endgame

1. (Johnson and Moggridge 1978), 554.

2. (Heyde 1998), 206; *Le Figaro*, 22 June 1931, 1; *Le Figaro*, 23 June 1931, 3 (revue de la presse); *Le Temps*, 22 June 1931, 1 (bulletin du jour); *Le Figaro*, 25 June 1931, 5 (revue de la presse); FRUS, 1931, Volume 1, 44.

3. FRUS, 1931, Volume 1, 46; Castle, Diary, 23 June 1931, quoted in (Wala 2001), 176.

4. FRUS, 1931, Volume 1, 63.

5. FRUS, 1931, Volume 1, 62–5; (Bennett 1962), 173–4.

6. FRUS, 1931, Volume 1, 62; ADAP, Serie B, Volume XVII, 481–3.

7. FRUS, 1931, Volume 1, 82: Edge to Acting Secretary of State; ADAP, Serie B, Volume XVII, 502–5.

8. FRUS, 1931, Volume 1, 66, 83.

9. FRUS, 1931, Volume 1, 42–3.

10. (Bennett 1962), 170–2.
11. (Heyde 1998), 213; FRUS, 1931, Volume 1, 83.
12. Quoted in (Heyde 1998), 182.
13. e.g. (Eichengreen 1992). Cf. critique by (Tooze 2014), 496.
14. FRUS, 1931, Volume 1, 83–4. Cf. (Bennett 1962), 183.
15. (Heyde 1998), 217.
16. (Heyde 1998), 220–1.
17. FRUS, 1931, Volume 1, 132; (Bennett 1962), 189–99.
18. Hoover, Public Papers, 672; (Pünder 1961), 154.
19. (Bennett 1962), 176.
20. (Bennett 1962), 176; Hoover, Public Papers, 672–3; FRUS, 1931, Volume 1, 160–1.
21. Schäffer, Diary, 6 July 1931; (Pünder 1961), 103.
22. (Bennett 1962), 176.
23. AdR, Brüning I, 1288–9; (Luther 1964), 178: On Friday, 26 June 1931, the Reichsbank lost RM 25 million. On Saturday, 27 June 1931, the loss amounted to RM 45 million.
24. (Luther 1964), 173–4; (Born 1967), 90.
25. AdR, Brüning I, 1264–8, 1281. (Priester 1932), 37, 43–4; (Born 1967), 85. The rumour was first rejected: e.g. VZ, 7 July 1931, morning edition, 1. The leak came from Deutsche Bank.
26. (Bähr and Rudolph 2011), 30 and 72; (Luther 1964), 179; AdR, Brüning I, 1295.
27. (Maurer, Wengst, and Heideking 1980), 733–40. AdR, Brüning I, 1292–4 and 1301–2. Cf. (Pünder 1961), 154; The Times, 8 July 1931, 14; The Economist, 11 July 1931, 61–2.
28. (Luther 1964), 184–5.
29. (Brüning 1970), 310; (Pünder 1961), 157–8; (Maurer, Wengst, and Heideking 1980), 825–42.
30. Schäffer, Diary, 10 July 1931.
31. (Maurer, Wengst, and Heideking 1980), 740–6.
32. (Maurer, Wengst, and Heideking 1980), 740–6. Cf. (Pünder 1961), 159; (James 1986), 313–14; (Pünder 1961), 159.
33. Schäffer, Diary, 11 July 1931; AdR, Brüning I, 1323–4 (footnote 6).
34. AdR, Brüning I, 1323–4.
35. (Maurer, Wengst, and Heideking 1980), 749–50; AdR, Brüning I, 1326 (footnote 13); (Pünder 1961), 159–61; (Luther 1964), 188–9; (Born 1967), 95–8.
36. AdR, Brüning I, 1329 and 1333; (Priester 1932), 60.
37. AdR, Brüning I, 1334–7; Schäffer, Diary, 12 July 1931; FRUS, 1931, Volume 1, 250–1; (Born 1967), 86, 95, and 100; (Burhop 2011), 22–3.

38. AdR, Brüning I, 1334–7; (Brüning 1970), 317.
39. AdR, Brüning I, 1338–44.
40. (Brüning 1970), 317–18. Cf. Schäffer, Diary, 12 July 1931, and (Priester 1932), 70–2.
41. Schäffer, Diary, 12 July 1931; AdR, Brüning I, 1340.
42. AdR, Brüning I, 1341; (Schacht 1953), 360–2.
43. AdR, Brüning I, 1342; (Maurer, Wengst, and Heideking 1980), 750–1.
44. AdR, Brüning I, 1342; Schäffer, Diary, 12 July 1931.
45. (Priester 1932), 75; (Pünder 1961), 161; AdR, Brüning I, 1342.
46. *The Times*, 13 July 1931, 12; (Luther 1964), 193.

Chapter 10: The Rise of Hitler

1. (Schäffer 2008), 47–8; Schäffer, Diary, 13 July 1931.
2. (Priester 1932), 77; (Pünder 1961), 162; Schäffer, Diary, 13 July 1931; (Brüning 1970), 320; (Schäffer 2008), 48.
3. AdR, Brüning I, 1348–52.
4. AdR, Brüning I, 1352–3; Schäffer, Diary, 13 July 1931.
5. AdR, Brüning I, 1356–66; (Accominotti and Eichengreen 2016); *The Economist*, 19 July 1931, 102.
6. DBFP 1919–39, Second Series, Volume 2, 1931, No. 225.
7. (Bähr and Rudolph 2011), 79–110; (James 2013), 126–7; Royal Institute of International Affairs, Survey 1931, 87.
8. (Heyde 1998), 321.
9. (Eichengreen 2008), 82.
10. (Balderston 1993), 2; (Balderston 2002), 79; (Ritschl 2013), 131; GDP figures: The Maddison-Project, <http://www.ggdc.net/maddison/maddison-project/home.htm> (2013 version). On the question of devaluation see (Straumann 2009).
11. (Toynbee 1932), 1, 59, and 60.
12. (Herbert 2014), 272–3.
13. (Evans 2003), 224; (Herbert 2014), 280–3. For a biographical approach to Hitler see (Kershaw 1999), (Longerich 2015), and (Ullrich 2016).
14. Hitler: Reden, Schriften, Anordnungen: Februar 1925 bis Januar 1933, Band IV, Teil 2, Dok. 9, 35–6. The interview was published on 15 July 1931 in *The New York Herald*, Paris.
15. Hitler: Reden, Schriften, Anordnungen: Februar 1925 bis Januar 1933, Band IV, Teil 2, Dok. 13, 43–4. (Völkischer Beobachter, 1 August 1931).
16. Survey of International Affairs 1931, 322.

17. Hitler: Reden, Schriften, Anordnungen: Februar 1925 bis Januar 1933, Band IV, Teil 2, Dok. 46, 134–58. (Völkischer Beobachter, 16 August 1931).
18. (Fröhlich 2005), 56 (14 July 1931).

Epilogue

1. Quoted in (Wandel 1974), 250.
2. The 'secret history of the banking crisis' was written during the crisis. The report given to Wallenberg was written in 1934. Cf. (Wandel 1974), 193–6, 291–7.
3. (Schäffer 2008), 1.
4. Schäffer, Diary, 6 May 1931.
5. (Wandel 1974), 222.

REFERENCES

Accominotti, Olivier. 2012. 'London Merchant Banks, the Central European Panic, and the Sterling Crisis of 1931', *The Journal of Economic History*, 72: 1–43.

Accominotti, Olivier, and Barry Eichengreen. 2016. 'The Mother of All Sudden Stops: Capital Flows and Reversals in Europe, 1919–32', *The Economic History Review*, 69: 469–92.

Akten der Reichskanzlei: Die Kabinette Brüning I und II, edited by Tilman Koops, Boppard am Rhein: Boldt, 1982. (Abbreviation: AdR, Brüning)

Akten der Reichskanzlei: Das Kabinett Müller II, edited by Martin Vogt, Boppard am Rhein: Harald Boldt, 1970. (Abbreviation: AdR, Müller)

Akten zur deutschen Auswärtigen Politik, 1918–1945: Aus dem Archiv des deutschen Auswärtigen Amtes. Serie B: 1925–1933. Göttingen: Vandenhoeck & Ruprecht, 1966–83. (Abbreviation: ADAP)

Bachmann, Ursula. 1996. *Reichskasse und öffentlicher Kredit in der Weimarer Republik 1924–1932* (P. Lang: Frankfurt am Main, New York).

Bähr, Johannes, and Bernd Rudolph. 2011. *Finanzkrisen 1931, 2008* (Piper: München).

Balderston, Theo. 1993. *The Origins and Course of the German Economic Crisis: November 1923 to May 1932* (Haude & Spener: Berlin).

Balderston, Theo. 2002. *Economics and Politics in the Weimar Republic* (Cambridge University Press: Cambridge, New York).

Bennett, Edward W. 1962. *Germany and the Diplomacy of the Financial Crisis, 1931* (Harvard University Press: Cambridge, Mass.).

Borchardt, Knut. 1991. *Perspectives on Modern German Economic History and Policy* (Cambridge University Press: Cambridge, New York).

Bordo, Michael, and Harold James. 2015. 'Capital Flows and Domestic and International Order: Trilemmas from Macroeconomics to Political Economy and International Relations', *NBER Working Paper 21017*.

Born, Karl Erich. 1967. *Die deutsche Bankenkrise 1931* (Piper: München).

Bromhead, Alan de, Barry Eichengreen, and Kevin O'Rourke. 2013. 'Political Extremism in the 1920s and 1930s: Do German Lessons Generalize?', *The Journal of Economic History*, 73: 371–406.

Brown, Brendan. 1988. *Monetary Chaos in Europe* (Croom Helm: London, New York).

Brüning, Franziska. 2010. *La France et le chancelier Brüning: imaginaire et politique, 1930–1932* (Éditions universitaires de Dijon: Dijon).

Brüning, Heinrich. 1970. *Memoiren 1918–1934* (Deutsche Verlags-Anstalt: Stuttgart).

Burhop, Carsten. 2011. 'The Historiography of the 1931 Crisis in Germany.' In *Jahrbuch für Wirtschaftsgeschichte/Economic History Yearbook*, 52 (2): 9.

Burke, Bernard V. 1994. *Ambassador Frederic Sackett and the Collapse of the Weimar Republic, 1930–1933: The United States and Hitler's Rise to Power* (Cambridge University Press: Cambridge, New York).

Büttner, Ursula. 2008. *Weimar: die überforderte Republik 1918–1933: Leistung und Versagen in Staat, Gesellschaft, Wirtschaft und Kultur* (Klett-Cotta: Stuttgart).

Crafts, Nicholas, and Peter Fearon. 2010. 'Lessons from the 1930s Great Depression', *Oxford Review of Economic Policy*, 26: 285–317.

Curtius, Julius. 1948. *Sechs Jahre Minister der Deutschen Republik* (C. Winter: Heidelberg).

Curtius, Julius. 1950. *Der Young-Plan; Entstellung und Wahrheit* (F. Mittelbach: Stuttgart).

Documents on British Foreign Policy 1919–1939. 1946–1984. Edited by E. L. Woodward et al., London: Her Majesty's Stationery Office. (Abbreviation: DBFP)

Eichengreen, Barry J. 1992. *Golden Fetters: The Gold Standard and the Great Depression, 1919–1939* (Oxford University Press: New York).

Eichengreen, Barry J. 2008. *Globalizing Capital: A History of the International Monetary System* (Princeton University Press: Princeton).

Eichengreen, Barry J. 2015. *Hall of Mirrors: The Great Depression, the Great Recession, and the Uses—and Misuses—of History* (Oxford University Press: New York).

Enquête-Ausschuss. 1929. *Die Reichsbank* (Mittler: Berlin).

Evans, Richard J. 2003. *The Coming of the Third Reich* (A. Lane: London).

Feinstein, C. H., Peter Temin, and Gianni Toniolo. 1997. *The European Economy between the Wars* (Oxford University Press: Oxford, New York).

Feldman, Gerald D. 1993. *The Great Disorder: Politics, Economics, and Society in the German Inflation, 1914–1924* (Oxford University Press: New York).

Feldman, Gerald D. 1994. 'Jakob Goldschmidt, the History of the Banking Crisis of 1931, and the Problem of Freedom of Manoeuvre in the Weimar Economy', in Christoph Buchheim, Michael Hutter, and Harold James (eds), *Zerrissene Zwischenkriegszeit: Wirtschaftshistorische Beiträge* (Nomos: Baden-Baden).

Ferguson, Thomas, and Peter Temin. 2003. 'Made in Germany: The German Currency Crisis of July 1931', *Research in Economic History*, 21: 1–53.

Ferguson, Thomas, and Peter Temin. 2004. 'Comment on "The German Twin Crisis of 1931"', *The Journal of Economic History*, 64: 872–6.

Fröhlich, Elke (ed.). 2004. *Die Tagebücher von Joseph Goebbels, Teil I: Aufzeichnungen 1923–1941* (K. G. Saur: München).

Fröhlich, Elke (ed.). 2005. *Die Tagebücher von Joseph Goebbels, Teil I: Aufzeichnungen* (K. G. Saur: München).

Fromm, Bella. 1990. *Blood and Banquets: A Berlin Social Diary* (Carol Pub. Group: New York).

Galofré-Vilà, Gregori, Christopher M. Meissner, Martin McKee, and David Stuckler. 2017. 'Austerity and the Rise of the Nazi Party', *NBER Working Paper 24106*.

Gomes, Leonard. 2010. *German Reparations, 1919–1932: A Historical Survey* (Palgrave Macmillan: Basingstoke).

Hantke, M. A. X., and Mark Spoerer. 2010. 'The Imposed Gift of Versailles: The Fiscal Effects of Restricting the Size of Germany's Armed Forces, 1924–9', *The Economic History Review*, 63: 849–64.

Hardach, Gerd. 1976. *Weltmarktorientierung und relative Stagnation: Währungspolitik in Deutschland 1924–1931* (Duncker und Humblot: Berlin).

Herbert, Ulrich. 2014. *Geschichte Deutschlands im 20. Jahrhundert* (C. H. Beck: München).

Hesse, Jan-Otmar, Roman Köster, and Werner Plumpe. 2015. *Die Grosse Depression: Die Weltwirtschaftskrise 1929–1939* (Bundeszentrale für politische Bildung: Bonn).

Heyde, Philipp. 1998. *Das Ende der Reparationen: Deutschland, Frankreich und der Youngplan 1929–1932* (F. Schöningh: Paderborn).

Holtfrerich, Carl-Ludwig. 1986. *The German Inflation 1914–1923: Causes and Effects in International Perspective* (W. de Gruyter: Berlin).

Hömig, Herbert. 2000. *Brüning: Kanzler in der Krise der Republik: Eine Weimarer Biographie* (Schöningh: Paderborn).

Irwin, Douglas A. 2011. *Peddling Protectionism: Smoot–Hawley and the Great Depression* (Princeton University Press: Princeton).

James, Harold. 1984. 'The Causes of the German Banking Crisis of 1931', *The Economic History Review*, 37: 68–87.

James, Harold. 1985. *The Reichsbank and Public Finance in Germany, 1924–1933: A Study of the Politics of Economics during the Great Depression* (F. Knapp: Frankfurt am Main).

James, Harold. 1986. *The German Slump: Politics and Economics, 1924–1936* (Clarendon Press, Oxford University Press: Oxford, New York).

James, Harold. 2009. *The Creation and Destruction of Value: The Globalization Cycle* (Harvard University Press: Cambridge, Mass.).

James, Harold. 2013. 'The 1931 Central European Banking Crisis Revisited', in Hartmut Berghoff, Jürgen Kocka, and Dieter Ziegler (eds), *Business in the Age of Extremes: Essays in Modern German and Austrian Economic History* (Cambridge University Press: Cambridge).

James, Harold. 2014. 'International Capital Movements and the Global Order', in Larry Neal and Jeffrey G. Williamson (eds), *The Cambridge History of Capitalism*, volume 2 (Cambridge University Press: Cambridge).

Johnson, Elizabeth, and Donald Moggridge (eds). 1978. *The Collected Writings of John Maynard Keynes* (Cambridge University Press: Cambridge).

Kershaw, Ian. 1999. *Hitler* (W. W. Norton: New York).

Kershaw, Ian. 2015. *To Hell and back: Europe, 1914–1949* (Viking: New York).

Kindleberger, Charles P. 1973. *The World in Depression, 1929–1939* (Allen Lane: London).

Knipping, Franz. 1987. *Deutschland, Frankreich und das Ende der Locarno-Ära 1928–1931: Studien zur internationalen Politik in der Anfangsphase der Weltwirtschaftskrise* (R. Oldenbourg: München).

Knortz, Heike. 2010. *Wirtschaftsgeschichte der Weimarer Republik: Eine Einführung in Ökonomik und Gesellschaft der ersten Deutschen Republik* (Vandenhoeck & Ruprecht: Göttingen).

Kolb, Eberhard. 2003. *Gustav Stresemann* (C. H. Beck: München).

Kopper, Christopher. 2006. *Hjalmar Schacht: Aufstieg und Fall von Hitlers mächtigstem Bankier* (Hanser: München).

Leith-Ross, Frederick. 1968. *Money Talks: Fifty Years of International Finance. The Autobiography of Sir Frederick Leith-Ross* (Hutchinson: London).

Link, Werner. 1970. *Die amerikanische Stabilisierungspolitik in Deutschland 1921–32* (Droste Verlag: Düsseldorf).

Lohe, Eilert. 1961. *Der Bruch der Grossen Koalition und die Anfänge der Regierung Brüning im Urteil englischer Diplomaten: Eine Untersuchung der britischen Gesandtschaftsberichte über Fragen der deutschen Innen- und Aussenpolitik von der Bildung des Kabinetts Brüning bis zur Begegnung in Chequers, (März 1930—Juni 1931)* (Druck E. Reuter-Gesellschaft: Berlin).

Longerich, Peter. 2015. *Hitler: Biographie* (Siedler: München).

Luther, Hans. 1964. *Vor dem Abgrund, 1930–1933; Reichsbankpräsident in Krisenzeiten* (Propyläen Verlag: Berlin).

Macher, Flora. 2015. 'The Causes of the Austrian Crisis of 1931', *mimeo LSE*.

MacMillan, Margaret. 2001. *Peacemakers: The Paris Conference of 1919 and its Attempt to End War* (J. Murray: London).

McNeil, William C. 1986. *American Money and the Weimar Republic: Economics and Politics on the Eve of the Great Depression* (Columbia University Press: New York).

Marcus, Nathan. 2011. 'Credibility, Confidence and Capital: Austrian Reconstruction and the Collapse of Global Finance: 1921–1931', PhD thesis New York University.

Marks, Sally. 1978. 'The Myths of Reparations', *Central European History*, 11: 231–55.

Maurer, Ilse. 1973. 'Reichsfinanzen und Grosse Koalition: Zur Geschichte des Reichskabinetts Müller (1928–1930)', Originally presented as the author's thesis, Heidelberg.

Maurer, Ilse, Udo Wengst, and Jürgen Heideking (eds). 1980. *Politik und Wirtschaft in der Krise 1930–1932: Quellen zur Ära Brüning* (Droste: Düsseldorf).

Meissner, Otto. 1950. *Staatssekretär unter Ebert, Hindenburg, Hitler: Der Schicksalsweg des deutschen Volkes von 1918–1945, wie ich ihn erlebte* (Hoffmann & Campe: Hamburg).

Menken, Jules. 1931. 'The German Economy and Reparations', *Survey of International Affairs 1930*.

Mertz-Rychner, Claudia (ed.). 1991. *Briefwechsel Hugo von Hofmannsthal, Carl Jacob Burckhardt* (Fischer: Frankfurt).

Monnet, François. 1993. *Refaire la République: André Tardieu, une dérive réactionnaire (1876–1945)* (Fayard: Paris).

Morsey, Rudolf. 1975. *Zur Entstehung, Authentizität und Kritik von Brünings 'Memoiren 1918–1934'* (Westdeutscher Verlag: Opladen).

Moulton, Harold G., and Leo Pasvolsky. 1932. *War Debts and World Prosperity* (The Brookings Institution: New York).

Mouré, Kenneth. 1991. *Managing the Franc Poincaré: Economic Understanding and Political Constraint in French Monetary Policy, 1928–1936* (Cambridge University Press: Cambridge, New York).

Papers relating to the Foreign Relations of the United States 1930–1934, Washington, DC: United States Government Printing Office, 1945–51. (Abbreviation: FRUS)

Partnoy, Frank. 2009. *The Match King: Ivar Kreuger, the Financial Genius behind a Century of Wall Street Scandals* (PublicAffairs: New York).

Patch, William L. 1998. *Heinrich Brüning and the Dissolution of the Weimar Republic* (Cambridge University Press: Cambridge, New York).

Polanyi, Karl. 1944. *The Great Transformation* (Farrar & Rinehart: New York).

Ponticelli, Jacopo, and Hans-Joachim Voth. 2012. 'Austerity and Anarchy: Budget Cuts and Social Unrest in Europe, 1919–2009', *CEPR discussion paper*.

Priester, Hans Erich. 1932. *Das geheimnis des 13. juli* (Georg Stilke: Berlin).

Pünder, Hermann. 1961. *Politik in der Reichskanzlei: Aufzeichnungen aus den Jahren 1929–1932* (Deutsche Verlags-Anstalt: Stuttgart).

Pyta, Wolfram. 2007. *Hindenburg: Herrschaft zwischen Hohenzollern und Hitler* (Siedler: München).

Rappleye, Charles. 2016. *Herbert Hoover in the White House: The Ordeal of the Presidency* (Simon & Schuster: New York).

Ritschl, Albrecht. 2002. *Deutschlands Krise und Konjunktur 1924–1934: Binnenkonjunktur, Auslandsverschuldung und Reparationsproblem zwischen Dawes-Plan und Transfersperre* (Akademie Verlag: Berlin).

Ritschl, Albrecht. 2013. 'Reparations, Deficits, and Debt Default: The Great Depression in Germany', in Nicholas Crafts and Peter Fearon (eds), *The Great Depression of the 1930s: Lessons for Today* (Oxford University Press: Oxford).

Ritschl, Albrecht, and Samad Sarferaz. 2014. 'Currency versus Banking in the Financial Crisis of 1931', *International Economic Review*, 55: 349–73.

Rödder, Andreas. 1996. *Stresemanns Erbe: Julius Curtius und die deutsche Aussenpolitik, 1929–1931* (Ferdinand Schöningh: Paderborn).

Rodrik, Dani. 2011. *The Globalization Paradox: Democracy and the Future of the World Economy* (W. W. Norton & Company: New York).

Schacht, Hjalmar Horace Greeley. 1953. *76 Jahre meines Lebens* (Kindler und Schiermeyer: Bad Wörishofen).

Schäffer, Hans. 1967. *Carl Melchior: Ein Buch des Gedenkens und der Freundschaft* (J. C. B. Mohr (Paul Siebeck): Tübingen).

Schäffer, Hans. 2008. *Marcus Wallenberg und die Deutsche Bankenkrise 1931* (Verlag Edmund Steinschulte: Wiesbaden).

Schmidt, Paul. 1949. *Statist auf diplomatischer Bühne, 1923–45* (Athenäum-Verlag: Bonn).

Schnabel, Isabel. 2004a. 'The German Twin Crisis of 1931', *The Journal of Economic History*, 64: 822–71.

Schnabel, Isabel. 2004b. 'Reply to Thomas Ferguson and Peter Temin's "Comment on 'The German Twin Crisis of 1931'"', *The Journal of Economic History*, 64: 877–8.

Schubert, Aurel. 1991. *The Credit-Anstalt Crisis of 1931* (Cambridge University Press: Cambridge, New York).

Schuker, Stephen A. 1988. *American 'Reparations' to Germany, 1919–33: Implications for the Third-World Debt Crisis* (International Finance Section, Dept. of Economics, Princeton University: Princeton).

Schulz, Gerhard. 1992. *Zwischen Demokratie und Diktatur: Verfassungspolitik und Reichsreform in der Weimarer Republik* (W. de Gruyter: Berlin, New York).

Schwerin-Krosigk, Lutz. 1951. *Es geschah in Deutschland; Menschenbilder unseres Jahrhunderts* (Rainer Wunderlich Verlag: Tübingen).

Schwerin von Krosigk, Lutz. 1974. *Staatsbankrott: Die Geschichte der Finanzpolitik des Deutschen Reiches von 1920 bis 1945* (Musterschmidt: Göttingen).

Shamir, Haim. 1989. *Economic Crisis and French Foreign Policy, 1930–1936* (E. J. Brill: Leiden, New York).

Somary, Felix. 1931. 'The American and European Economic Depressions and their Political Consequences', *International Affairs*, 10: 160–76.

Somary, Felix. 1932. *Ursachen der Krise* (J. C. B Mohr (Paul Siebeck): Tübingen).

Somary, Felix. 1986. *The Raven of Zürich: The Memoirs of Felix Somary* (C. Hurst & Co., St Martin's Press: London, New York).

Somary, Wolfgang. 1994. 'Vorwort', in Felix Somary (ed.), *Erinnerungen eines politischen Meteorologen* (Matthes & Seitz: München).

Straumann, Tobias. 2009. 'Rule rather than Exception: Brüning's Fear of Devaluation in Comparative Perspective', *Journal of Contemporary History*, 44: 603–17.

Straumann, Tobias. 2013. 'Einführung', in Wolfgang Somary (ed.), *Felix Somary: Erinnerungen an mein Leben* (Verlag Neue Zürcher Zeitung: Zurich).

Straumann, Tobias, Peter Kugler, and Florian Weber. 2017. 'How the German Crisis of 1931 Swept across Europe: A Comparative View from Stockholm', *The Economic History Review*, 70: 224–47.

Tabouis, Geneviève. 1958. *Vingt ans de suspense diplomatique* (Albin Michel: Paris).

Temin, Peter, and David Vines. 2013. *The Leaderless Economy: Why the World Economic System Fell apart and How to Fix it* (Princeton University Press: Princeton).

Toniolo, Gianni. 2005. *Central Bank Cooperation at the Bank for International Settlements, 1930–1973* (Cambridge University Press: Cambridge, New York).

Tooze, J. Adam. 2014. *The Deluge: The Great War, America and the Remaking of the Global Order, 1916–1931* (Viking Adult: New York).

Toynbee, Arnold. 1932. 'Part I. The World Crisis: (i) Annus Terribilis 1931', in Royal Institute of International Affairs (ed.), *Survey of International Affairs 1931* (Oxford University Press: London), 1–161.

Treviranus, Gottfried Reinhold. 1968. *Das Ende von Weimar: Heinrich Brüning und seine Zeit* (Econ-Verlag: Düsseldorf).

Ullrich, Volker. 2016. *Hitler: Ascent, 1889–1939* (Alfred A. Knopf: New York).

Unger, Gérard. 2005. *Aristide Briand* (Fayard: Paris).

Voth, Hans-Joachim. 2003. 'With a Bang, Not a Whimper: Pricking Germany's: Stockmarket Bubble in 1927 and the Slide into Depression', *Journal of Economic History*, 63: 65–99.

Wala, Michael. 2001. *Weimar und Amerika: Botschafter Friedrich von Prittwitz und Gaffron und die deutsch-amerikanischen Beziehungen von 1927 bis 1933* (F. Steiner: Stuttgart).

Wandel, Eckhard. 1974. *Hans Schäffer: Steuermann in wirtschaftlichen und politischen Krisen* (Deutsche Verlags-Anstalt: Stuttgart).

Wehler, Hans-Ulrich. 2003. *Vom Beginn des Ersten Weltkriegs bis zur Gründung der beiden deutschen Staaten, 1914–1949* (C. H. Beck: München).

Wicker, Elmus. 1996. *The Banking Panics of the Great Depression* (Cambridge University Press: Cambridge, New York).

Winkler, Heinrich August. 2000. *Der Lange Weg nach Westen* (Beck: München).

Wolf, Nikolaus. 2010. 'Europe's Great Depression: Coordination Failure after the First World War', *Oxford Review of Economic Policy*, 26: 339–69.

Zweig, Stefan. 2013. *The World of Yesterday* (University of Nebraska Press: Lincoln, Nebr.).

PICTURE CREDITS

Maps

Figures

Illustrations

11. Senator-Elect Frederick M. Sackett of Kentucky, 12/11/24. Photograph. Retrieved from the Library of Congress.
12. Bundesarchiv, Koblenz.
13. Bain News Service, P. J. Ramsay MacDonald. Retrieved from the Library of Congress.
14. Herbert Hoover. Retrieved from the Library of Congress.
15. Ullstein bild Dtl/Getty.
16. Bundesarchiv, Koblenz.

INDEX